ISBN 978-1-331-86061-7
PIBN 10243342

1 MONTH OF
FREE
READING

at

www.ForgottenBooks.com

By purchasing this book you are eligible for one month membership to ForgottenBooks.com, giving you unlimited access to our entire collection of over 1,000,000 titles via our web site and mobile apps.

To claim your free month visit:

www.forgottenbooks.com/free243342

English
Français
Deutsche
Italiano
Español
Português

www.forgottenbooks.com

Mythology Photography **Fiction**
Fishing Christianity **Art** Cooking
Essays Buddhism Freemasonry
Medicine **Biology** Music **Ancient**
Egypt Evolution Carpentry Physics
Dance Geology **Mathematics** Fitness
Shakespeare **Folklore** Yoga Marketing
Confidence Immortality Biographies
Poetry **Psychology** Witchcraft
Electronics Chemistry History **Law**
Accounting **Philosophy** Anthropology
Alchemy Drama Quantum Mechanics
Atheism Sexual Health **Ancient History**
Entrepreneurship Languages Sport
Paleontology Needlework Islam
Metaphysics Investment Archaeology
Parenting Statistics Criminology
Motivational

THE LIFE AND TIMES OF
GILBERT SHELDON

SOMETIME WARDEN OF ALL SOULS COLLEGE, OXFORD;
BISHOP OF LONDON; ARCHBISHOP OF CANTERBURY:
AND CHANCELLOR OF THE UNIVERSITY OF OXFORD

BY

VERNON STALEY

RECTOR OF ICKFORD, BUCKS AND OXON.
HON. CANON OF THE CATHEDRAL CHURCH OF ST. ANDREW, INVERNESS

Qui vixit non sibi sed bono publico

LONDON
GARDNER, DARTON & CO. LD.
3 & 4, PATERNOSTER BUILDINGS, E.C.
AND 44, VICTORIA STREET, S.W.

GILBERT SHELDON

From a photo by Hills & Saunders, from the oil painting in the

THE LIFE AND TIMES OF
GILBERT SHELDON

SOMETIME WARDEN OF ALL SOULS COLLEGE, OXFORD;
BISHOP OF LONDON; ARCHBISHOP OF CANTERBURY;
AND CHANCELLOR OF THE UNIVERSITY OF OXFORD

BY

RECTOR OF ICKFORD, BUCKS AND OXON.
HON. CANON OF THE CATHEDRAL CHURCH OF ST. ANDREW, INVERNESS

Qui vixit non sibi sed bono publico

LONDON

3 & 4, PATERNOSTER BUILDINGS, E.C.
AND 44, VICTORIA STREET, S.W.

PREFACE

Soon after my institution to the benefice once held by Gilbert Sheldon, I formed a purpose and indulged a hope that, in due time, I might be able to do something to place in true historical position the eminent English ecclesiastic, who more than two and a half centuries ago was my predecessor as Rector of Ickford. And this intention has been strengthened by the knowledge that, incredible though it may seem, no Life of Sheldon has hitherto been written. The prosecution of my studies and researches in regard to Sheldon and his career has again and again filled me with surprise and amazement at such an omission. Whilst men, conspicuously his inferiors in personal character, ability, activity, munificence, and influence in the Church of England since the Reformation, have found ready and capable biographers, Gilbert Sheldon has been unaccountably neglected, and even deserted by those of his own way of thinking and working. And yet, as I hope to demonstrate in the following pages, from the death of Laud to the primacy of Sancroft—a most important and eventful period of English Church history—Sheldon stands out as the most eminent and capable Churchman of the time covered by the Great Rebellion and the Restoration. His position and influence in the Church only finds its parallel in that occupied by Clarendon in the State. To Sheldon and Clarendon was committed the delicate and responsible task of reorganising and re-establishing the English Church and Nation, after the convulsion and upheaval of the Commonwealth—a task which, when we survey the whole complicated situation created by the Revolution, and recognise the corrupt state of the Court at the Restoration, fills the mind with dismay by its intricacy and vastness. The variety and balance of conflicting interests to be reconciled, the heat to which the party feelings of the religious world had risen, with which Clarendon and Sheldon had to contend, defy adequate description. As Moses the lawgiver and Aaron the priest of the ancient Church of Israel worked side by side, mutually assisting each other in their respective spheres of labour, so it was with Clarendon and Sheldon at the Restoration.

And yet, as I have said, no complete record of

the life and deeds of Gilbert Sheldon exists!
The nearest attempt in the way of collecting
materials for such a biography of this eminent
man is found in the admirable work, *Worthies
of All Souls*, written by Mr. Montagu Burrows,
sometime Chichele Professor of Modern History
in the University of Oxford, which was published
by Messrs. Macmillan & Co. in the year 1874.
As a Fellow of all Souls, the College of which
Sheldon was successively Fellow and Master
until his expulsion at the Great Rebellion, Mr.
Burrows naturally wrote of Sheldon with reverence
and appreciation, and, as far as I am able to
judge, with impartiality. To his *Worthies of All
Souls* I am greatly indebted for information upon
certain periods of Sheldon's career. My authority for the historical statements made in the
earliest pages of this work is Anthony à Wood's
Athenæ Oxonienses, second edition, corrected and
enlarged, Lond., 1721, vol. ii.

In writing this Life of Archbishop Sheldon,
my object has been to refer to and to quote the
writings of his contemporaries. To this end I
have made use of the works of Lord Clarendon,
his life-long friend, with whom he co-operated in
the reconstruction of Church and State under
King Charles II—John Evelyn, Samuel Pepys,

Anthony à Wood, and William Dugdale—all of whom were contemporary with Sheldon. The diaries of the last-named four persons have been of great service to me in accomplishing my task. All these men, Evelyn perhaps excepted, knew Gilbert Sheldon personally. The value of their testimony is therefore obvious.

In the following pages I have found it impossible to treat of Sheldon's Life in strictly chronological order, for the reason that, throughout his career in manhood, he held *contemporaneously* two or three positions—first, as Chaplain-in-Ordinary to King Charles I, Fellow and Warden of All Souls College, Oxford, Rector of Hackney, Ickford, Oddington, and Newington ; then, as Dean of the Chapel Royal, Master of the Savoy Hospital, and Bishop of London ; and, finally, Archbishop of Canterbury, and Chancellor of the University of Oxford. I have therefore thought it best to divide the Life into two main sections—his career before and up to the time of the Restoration, and that after the Restoration.

This attempt to compile the Life of Gilbert Sheldon has afforded me genuine satisfaction— the satisfaction of having been permitted to make some effort and attempt to rescue the memory of the character and actions of a good and great man from neglect, ingratitude, detraction, and misrepresentation—and, I feel constrained to add, from *malicious* misrepresentation at the hands of unscrupulous enemies. I venture to think thàt what I have set down in the concluding chapter of this work, in dealing with Sheldon's character and motives, will be considered a sufficient justification for so grave and sweeping an indictment. To clear this great servant of the English Church from obloquy, and to rehabilitate him in his true historical setting, has been a grateful task to one who has the privilege of living in the house he once occupied, of ministering in the same church in which for many years he ministered, and of moving daily in the scenes with which he was once so familiar before the Great Rebellion. As to how far I have been successful, I must leave my readers to judge from a perusal of the following pages. I have honestly tried to make the *amende honorable*, and an act of reparation for the palpable injustice done in the past to the great and inspiring memory of Gilbert Sheldon.

I desire to express my grateful sense of obligation to the late Mrs. Sherwood Hale of Alderley, Gloucestershire, for permission to use freely the magnificent library of Alderley House, where, during a long visit, nearly the whole of the following pages were written. This library is singularly rich in literature of the age of Gilbert Sheldon, as I think my Life of Sheldon shows. I also have to thank Dr. J. Wickham Legg, Oxford, and the Rev. Cyril T. H. Walker, Oxford, for researches of value in the Bodleian Library; also to the Rev. J. R. Pendlebury, Rector of Newington, Wallingford, the Rev. T. L. Tudor Fitzjohn, Rector of Oddington, Islip, Oxon—the present occupiers of Gilbert Sheldon's parishes—for most kind replies to my enquiries about his tenancy of their benefices; also to the Rev. E. H. Birley, Rector of Ellastone, Ashbourne, for much valuable information concerning the Sheldon family, and the copy of the entry of Gilbert Sheldon's baptism, transcribed from the old register. To the Rev. H. M. Lake, Curate-in-Charge of St. Margaret's, Upper Norwood, for his visit to Croydon Church, and the procuring of the photograph of Archbishop Sheldon's monument in that church.

The photographs from which the Plates contained in this volume are reproduced are taken by the following artists—Frontispiece, Hills and Saunders, Oxford; Plates facing pages 16, 22, 26, 96, 100, 224, F. Chadbone, Worminghall, Bucks; facing pages 32, 150, 154, 160, 164, 176,

180, 184, 208, A. H. Pitcher, Gloucester, by kind leave of Mrs. Sherwood Hale, of Alderley House, Wotton - under - Edge, Gloucestershire; facing page 192, C. H. Price, Croydon.

VERNON STALEY.

ICKFORD,
  Easter, 1913.

CONTENTS

PART I

SHELDON BEFORE THE RESTORATION

CHAPTER I

CHAPTER II

PART II

SHELDON AFTER THE RESTORATION

CHAPTER III

CHAPTER IV

CHAPTER V

CHAPTER VI

CHAPTER VII

CHAPTER VIII

CHAPTER IX

APPENDICES

ILLUSTRATIONS

In the Sheldonian Theatre, Oxford, attributed to Sir Peter Lely (A.D. 1618–80), born at Soest by Amersfoort, near Utrecht.

Malcolm, in his *Londinium Redivivum*, Lond. 1803, vol. i. p. 430, in describing the Charterhouse of his day, wrote: "On the East-wall, of the Governor's Room, Gilbert Sheldon, D.D., archbishop of Canterbury, in his robes, seated, upon a purple chair thrice fringed with gold. He rests an open book against his thigh, and holds a white handkerchief in his left hand, on the arm of the chair. The collegiate cap hurts the air of his face, which is shaded by chestnut hair; on his chin and lips are tufts of beard. He has heavy eyebrows, and not a very prepossessing countenance. We do not find in it an index to his exalted goodness and unbounded charities. A table covered with purple velvet supports a book and letter before him, and the background is formed by a portico. No name."

This is evidently the same portrait which now hangs in the Sheldonian Theatre, Oxford. The inscription runs:

Venerandam hanc ampliorimi Fundatoris
Propatici colendissimi Effigem: JUDITH et
MARIA Sheldon, DANIELIS filiae et cohaeredes:
In Aedibus SHELDONIANIS collocari F.
ix Kal. Feb. MDCCXXI.

Reproduction by photography of the Register of Baptisms, in Sheldon's handwriting, of the Parish Church of Ickford, for the years 1648, 1649, and 1650. These entries are of special interest; the first three entries in 1648 record baptisms during the six months when Sheldon was imprisoned by the Parliamentary Visitors of Oxford University. The whole of the entries shown relate to baptisms after the time of his ejection from the Wardenship of All Souls College, Oxford, and his supposed ejection from the benefice of Ickford. They seem to imply that Sheldon was not in fact ejected from Ickford till after the close of December 1650. For a discussion upon this point see the text of the present volume (part i., chapter i.).

expense, from plans of Christopher Wren, and opened 1669:
the views are, therefore, contemporary.   The Sheldonian Theatre
was Wren's first work of importance and made his name.

> Two views of the exterior of Old St. Paul's Cathedral, burnt to
> the ground in the Fire of London, A.D. 1666.   The prints are repro-
> duced from William Dugdale's *History of St. Paul's Cathedral in
> London*, Lond. 1658, *i.e.* but eight years before the Fire, and both
> were engraved by W. Hollar in 1657.   They are labelled respec-
> tively: (1) "Ecclesiæ Paulinæ Prospectus, qualis olim erat prius-
> quam ejus pyramis e cœlo tacta conflagraverat," (2) "Ecclesiæ
> Cathedralis S. Pauli, ab Oriente prospectus."   The first view
> shows the spire, which was destroyed by fire in 1561; also Inigo
> Jones' incongruous classic portico at the West end, added during
> the first half of the seventeenth century.

> The Lady Chapel of Old St. Paul's, with screen and elaborate
> rose-window.   Engraving by W. Hollar, 1657, in Dugdale's
> *History of St. Paul's Cathedral*, Lond.   1658, and labelled
> "Orientalis Partis Eccl. Cath. S. Pauli, prospectus interior."

> The Choir of modern St. Paul's Cathedral, looking West; from
> an engraving "published according to Act of Parliament 1754," for
> Stow's *Survey of the Cities of London and Westminster*, originally
> issued in 1598; reprinted, "corrected, improved, and very much
> enlarged" by John Strype in 1720.   Stow died in 1605.   This
> engraving shows the choir-screen surmounted by the organ, since
> removed; also the lectern, and pulpit with sounding board, stand-
> ing in the midst of the choir.
>
> "The Organ-Gallery, with four Stalls, two northward, and two
> southward therefrom, compose the west End (of the Quire).   The
> Organ-Case is magnificent and very ornamental, enriched with
> the carved Figures of *Cupids* under mantling *Terms*, and eight
> *Fames* standing at the Top of this Case, four looking eastward,
> and as many westward, each appearing near six Feet high: It
> is also enriched with Cherubims, Fruit, Leaves, &c., very lively
> represented, by that excellent Artist, Mr. *Gibon;* all which is
> elevated on eight beautiful fluted Columns of the *Corinthian*
> Order, of polished Marble, White veined with Blue, and the
> Organ-Pipes are very spacious and gilt with Gold, preserved from
> Dust, &c., with fine *Sashes*.   The north and south Sides of this

Choir have each thirty Stalls, besides the Bishop's Throne and
Seat on the south Side, and the Lord Mayor's on the north."—
Stow's *Survey of London*, 6th ed., Lond. 1754, Book iii. fol. 650.

"The clergy insisted on an enclosure of the choir, no doubt
partly for their own comfort and secluded dignity. Whether
Wren designed any screen, or to what height that screen was to
rise, does not appear. But he was compelled to submit, and,
contrary to his judgment, to place the organ-gallery and organ
upon the screen. The organ was the work of Bernard Smith;
it cost £2000."—Milman, *St. Paul's* (Murray: Lond. 1879),
pp. 79, 80.

In the year 1860, the return stalls, with the marble screen
were removed, and the organ placed in the second arch of the
north choir aisle : here it remained for ten years, when it was
moved to its present position, north and south of the choir. The
marble screen now forms porches to the north and south transepts
(see *The Guardian*, Oct. 11, 1912, p. 1284).

The Choir of modern St. Paul's Cathedral, looking East ; from
an engraving in Bernard Picart's *Ceremonies and Religious Customs'
of the Various Nations*, . . ., Lond. 1737, vol. vi. part i. This
view was engraved in 1736, and describes "La Communion des
Anglicans à Saint Paul," as inscribed at the foot of the Plate. The
pulpit as to design, sounding board, and position should be compared with that depicted in the previous Plate. Two lighted candles
are shown, standing on the holy table. This Plate is of special
interest, since it was alluded to, as evidence for the use of lighted
candles at the Communion, in daylight, by Archbishop Benson, in
the Bishop of Lincoln's Case of 1890: "It is remarkable that in
Picart's magnificent work there is a very large plate representing
The Communion of the Anglicans at St. Paul's, and that the Amster-
dam edition of 1726 has the lights unlit, but that the London
edition of the following year shows them lighted " (*The Bishop of
Lincoln's Case*, ed. E. S. Roscoe, Lond. 1891, pp. 168, 169).
Dr. Benson gives 1727 as the date of the London edition, whilst
the date of the edition from which a reproduction is here made is
1737, the Plate being engraved, as stated above, in 1736.

Archbishop Sheldon's tomb in Croydon Parish Church, erected
by his nephew, Sir Joseph Sheldon, sometime Lord Mayor of
London. The archbishop is shown with long hair, a mitre on his
head, bands below the chin, a close-fitting rochet, chimere with
full lawn sleeves attached to the arm-holes; in his hand is a
pastoral staff. The inscription is printed amongst the Appendices
to this volume. The monument was recently injured by fire, as
represented in the Plate. (From a photograph by C. H. Price,
Croydon.)

The Cloisters, with parts of the Guard Room and the Chapel of Lambeth Palace, from an old print. According to Lysons (*Environs of London*, i. 265), Archbishop Sheldon restored the galleries over the cloisters and adapted them to the purposes of a library, for the reception of Bancroft's books.

Communion Cup and Paten of silver, given by Gilbert Sheldon, when Bishop of London, to the Church of St. Nicholas, Ickford, Bucks. The Cup stands $9\frac{1}{8}$ inches high, the diameter of the lip is $5\frac{1}{2}$ inches, and the depth of the bowl is inside $5\frac{1}{2}$ inches. Round the lip outside is engraved : " Ex dono Gilberti Episcopi Londini nup Rectoris de Ickford in Com. Bucks." The Cup is of an extraordinary large size, and is capable of holding sufficient of the Sacred Element to communicate 150 persons or more. The date of the year letter is 1661. The size of the Cup must be considered in regard to the rubric in the Prayer Book.

> And note, that every parishioner shall communicate at the least three times in the year.

At the Restoration reception of the Holy Communion on the part of adults was regarded as a test of loyalty to Church and Crown. At the period of Sheldon's gift of this altar-plate, the number of adults in the parish of Ickford was probably from 100 to 150 : hence the large capacity of the Cup.

The Paten, used also as a cover to the Cup, rests on a circular foot ; it measures $6\frac{3}{4}$ inches in diameter at the surface, and stands $1\frac{3}{8}$ inches high. Under the base or foot is engraved, " Ickford Communion plate."

The hall-marks on both Cup and Paten are " R.E." (initials of maker) ; leopard's head crowned ; lion *passant ;* and " D " in old English type, on a shield, the year letter of A.D. 1661.

Weight : *Cup*, 23 oz. 10 dwt. 12 grs. ; *Cover*, 9 oz. 1 dwt. 3 grs. This is the weight recorded in the Ickford Register, Oct. 20, 1730.

Chronology of Gilbert Sheldon

BORN	June 19, 1598
BAPTIZED	June 26, 1598
COMMONER OF TRINITY COLLEGE, OXON .	1613
BACHELOR OF ARTS	Nov. 27, 1617
MASTER OF ARTS	May 20, 1620
ORDAINED	c. 1622
FELLOW OF ALL SOULS COLLEGE, OXON .	1622
BACHELOR OF DIVINITY	Nov. 11, 1628
VICAR OF HACKNEY	May 2, 1633
DOCTOR OF DIVINITY	June 25, 1634
CHAPLAIN TO KING CHARLES I . .	c. 1634
WARDEN OF ALL SOULS COLLEGE, OXON .	March, 1635
RECTOR OF ICKFORD	May 8, 1636
„ „ ODDINGTON	July 19, 1636
„ „ NEWINGTON	June 21, 1639
EJECTED FROM ALL SOULS, OXON . .	April 13, 1648
DEAN OF THE CHAPEL ROYAL . . .	1660
BISHOP OF LONDON	Oct. 28, 1660
ARCHBISHOP OF CANTERBURY . . .	Aug. 31, 1663
CHANCELLOR OF UNIVERSITY OF OXFORD	1667
DIED	Nov. 9, 1677

PART I

SHELDON BEFORE THE RESTORATION

THE LIFE AND TIMES OF
GILBERT SHELDON

CHAPTER I

GILBERT SHELDON'S EARLY CAREER

Birth—Family history—Baptism—Commoner of Trinity College, Oxford—Ordination—Fellow of All Souls College, Oxford—Domestic chaplain to Sir Thomas Coventry—Prebend of Gloucester Cathedral—Connection with Lord Clarendon—Vicar of Hackney—Chaplain-in-Ordinary to King Charles I—Warden of All Souls College, Oxford—Sheldon and Chillingworth—Rector of Ickford—Sheldon's entries in the Ickford Register—Church of St. Nicholas, Ickford—Sheldon, Rector of Oddington, and Rector of Newington.

GILBERT SHELDON was the youngest son of Roger Sheldon of Stanton, a village in the parish of Ellastone, in the county of Staffordshire,[1] where he was born on June 19, 1598. Anthony à Wood, in his *Athenæ Oxonienses*, states that he was born on July 19 of that year ; but in Sheldon's family Bible, now in the Bodleian Library, Oxford, the entry in handwriting is, " Gilb. Sheldon, borne June 19, 1598." As he was baptized on June 26,

[1] Near to Ashbourne, in the diocese of Lichfield.

Anthony à Wood is in error. The date of his birth thus falls within the closing years of the reign of Queen Elizabeth, and of the decade which is remarkable as being the period wherein English literature attained its loftiest height. It was the age of Richard Hooker, the first in time of our modern writers in prose; and of Edmund Spenser, the first Englishman, in Dean Church's opinion, to achieve a poetical work of the first order. Hooker's *Ecclesiastical Polity* was published in 1594; Spenser's *Faëry Queen* in 1590. Gilbert Sheldon belongs to that last quarter of the sixteenth century and the first half of the seventeenth century, in which the results of the former period, so singularly fruitful in eminent men, important events, and new and bold beginnings in the area of politics, philosophy, and religion, made themselves felt.

The Sheldons were an old Staffordshire family, and no doubt Gilbert Sheldon inherited some of those ample funds which later he contributed so lavishly to public objects in both Church and State. His Christian name was given to him at his baptism by Gilbert, seventh Earl of Shrewsbury (A.D. 1553–1616), in whose house Roger Sheldon was a menial servant. The Earl's interest in this last-born son of his dependant is somewhat remarkable ; it seems to point to some regard on the part of the Earl for an ancient family which had come down in the world—a family which was destined to produce a descendant who was to rise to the most exalted position in the Church. How little could Roger Sheldon and his wife have dreamed, as they stood by the font, that their last-born would become the chief adviser of King Charles I, the co-operator with Lord Clarendon in the reorganisation of the Church and State at the restoration of King Charles II, Bishop of London, and Archbishop of Canterbury! Yet so it came to pass. As to whether Roger Sheldon lived to see his son rising to fame, we know not. When a man by his own merits rises to eminence in the world— as once a peasant became pope—we judge his earlier by his later state, and not the reverse. We do not say, " This proves the archbishop to be no more than a pretentious peasant," but " This shows that even an unknown peasant may be a potential archbishop." For as Aristotle, once for all, laid down the broad principle—" The true nature of a thing is whatsoever it becomes, when the process of development is complete."

The old register of Ellastone-with-Stanton dates from A.D. 1538, and has been printed and published by the Staffordshire Parish Register Society. The entry of Gilbert Sheldon's baptism appears as follows—

"1598. Gylbarte ye sonn of Roger Sheldon and his wyffe was baptized the xxvith of June."

A note at the bottom of the page of the register, in a later hand, states, "This Gilbert Sheldon was made Archbishop of Canterbury in ye year 1663, died in ye year 1677."

In the same register are further entries relating to the Sheldons, as follows—

"Roger . . . ldon and Helen Woodcocke were married xxviith day of November 1592."

"Hughe the sonn of Roger Sheldon and his wiffe was baptized ye xiith of August (1593)."

"Ralphe the sonne of Roger Sheldon and his wiffe was baptized the first daye of August 1595."

"Ellen the wife of Mr. Roger Sheldon was buried the same day A^o p^o dict. (*i.e.* April 18, 1631)."

All these entries, including Gilbert's baptism, are marked with a cross (×), evidently to indicate the same family, and its importance. "Hughe" and "Ralphe" were Gilbert's brothers, and "Ellen" his mother. "Roger," married in 1592, was almost certainly Gilbert Sheldon's father.

There appears to be no entry of the burial of
Roger Sheldon, his father.

In the bedroom of a farm-house at Stanton is
a board, on which are written four lines in Latin,
recording the fact that Gilbert Sheldon was born
there—

> " Sheldonus ille Præsulam primus pater,
> Hos inter ortus aspicit lucem lares ;
> O ter beatam Stantonis villæ casam !
> Cui cuncta possunt invidere marmora." [1]

Of Gilbert Sheldon's boyhood and early education no information is forthcoming. We possess
no knowledge of the school to which he was sent
by his parents ; but we may safely assume that
his education was under the characteristic influ-
ences which marked the reign of King James I
(A.D. 1603–1625), and we may more safely assert
that he lived to become one of the most original
and worthy representatives of its spirit, as also
one of the most adequate exponents of its
religious and political ideas.

Towards the close of the year 1613, Gilbert,
then being but fifteen years of age, was admitted
a commoner of Trinity College, Oxford ; on
November 27, 1617, he took the degree of

---

[1] These lines are printed in Murray's *Handbook to Staffordshire*, &c.

Bachelor of Arts, and on May 20, 1620, the degree of Master of Arts. In 1622 he was elected Fellow of All Souls College, as we learn from Anthony à Wood,[1] of which college, later, he was destined to become one of its most distinguished wardens. Sheldon took his B.D. degree on November 11, 1628; and on June 25, 1634, he compounded for his D.D. degree.

About the year 1622 Sheldon received Holy Orders, and, later, was appointed to the office of domestic chaplain to the Lord Keeper of the Great Seal, Sir Thomas Coventry, who in 1633 gave him a prebend in Gloucester Cathedral. In *A New History of Gloucestershire*,[2] we find, under a list of Prebends and Prebendaries, "*Fourth Stall.*—Gilbert Sheldon, B.D., was installed the 26th of February, 1633." So great was the Lord Keeper's esteem for and confidence in Sheldon, that he employed him in various affairs relating to both Church and State, as we learn from Clarendon,[3] who was Sheldon's close friend all

[1] A. Wood, *Athenæ Oxonienses*, Lond., 1721, vol. ii. pp. 1162, 3.

[2] Printed at Cirencester, 1779, p. 168.

[3] Edward Hyde, born A.D. 1608, Chancellor of the Exchequer, A.D. 1642, in the latter year knighted and made privy councillor; author of *The History of the Great Rebellion*, undertaken with the approbation of King Charles I; Chancellor of the University of Oxford, 1660; raised to the peerage, 1660. On Lord Clarendon's banishment in 1667 the University of Oxford, with but one dissentient voice, elected Gilbert Sheldon, then Archbishop of Canterbury, to succeed Clarendon as Chancellor of the University.

through life. With prophetic vision Clarendon anticipated great honours and high preferment for Sheldon from early years. Sir Thomas Coventry, who had been advanced to the office of Lord Keeper of the Great Seal of England by King Charles I in 1625, and three years later dignified with the degree of a baron, recommended Gilbert Sheldon, his domestic chaplain, to the notice of the King, as "a person well versed in political affairs."

In a sidenote in Walker's account of Gilbert Sheldon, in his *Sufferings of the Clergy during the Great Rebellion*,[1] we read that, "May 2, 1633, Sheldon was also admitted to the vicarage of Hackney, in Middlesex." The reference to Sheldon's preferment to Hackney, void by the promotion of David Dolben to the bishopric of Bangor, verified at the Bodleian Library, is as follows—

Ric. Newcourt, Repertorium
Ecclesiasticum Parochiale Londinense, London,
Motte & Bateman, 1708, fol. vol. i. p. 620.
Vicarii.

*   *   *   *   *   *   *

Laud. (72 . 9 . Gilb. Sheldon, S.T.B. 2 . Maii 1633, per
promot. Daulben   Car. I. RA.
ad Episcopat. Bangor.   Jure Praerog.

---

[1] For this account in full, see Appendix II at the end of this work.

Sheldon was vicar of Hackney from 1633–36. His name appears twice in the record of the vestry meetings. The rector of Hackney, the Rev. H. Mosley, in a letter to the present writer, says, " Sheldon does not appear to have been a regular attendant, always sending the curate."

About 1634 Gilbert Sheldon became chaplain-in-ordinary to King Charles I, and, later, clerk of the closet ; and he was intended for the posts of Master of the Savoy Hospital and of Dean of Westminster, but the Great Rebellion hindered these preferments for a time.

Early in March 1635 Sheldon was elected Warden of All Souls College, Oxford, of which more will be said later. About this time he wrote some letters to William Chillingworth in reference to subscription to the Thirty-nine Articles, the latter having scruples in this matter. Chillingworth, celebrated for his controversial talents, was born at Oxford in 1602, William Laud, then Fellow of St. John's College, being his god-father. He fell under the influence of the famous Jesuit, John Fisher, who was then frequently at Oxford. Chillingworth, unable to answer the Jesuit's arguments on the necessity of an infallible living judge to decide matters of faith, was brought to

hold that this judge was to be found in the
Roman Church. Upon this he forsook the
Church of his baptism, and embraced the Roman
Catholic religion. Through the efforts of Laud,
and by his influence, Chillingworth was led to re-
consider his new position, and finally he returned
to the communion of the English Church. Sir
Thomas Coventry, Keeper of the Great Seal,
offered him preferment, but this he steadily
refused to accept, because his conscience would
not permit him to subscribe the Thirty-nine
Articles and parts of the Book of Common
Prayer. Eventually, Chillingworth saw his way
to subscribe the Articles in the sense that they
were to be regarded as articles of peace and union,
and not of belief or assent, as he formerly thought
them to be. This was also the sense attached to
subscription by Archbishop Laud, and his friend,
Gilbert Sheldon, who laboured to convince him
of it. It was no doubt Sheldon who at last
assured him upon this point. Several letters
passed between Chillingworth and Sheldon upon
the subject. To one of the letters of the former
Sheldon replied: " God forbid that I should
persuade any to do against his conscience : be it
in itself good or bad, it must be a sin to lie."
Chillingworth writes of " his much honoured

friend Dr. Sheldon," and addresses him as "Good Dr. Sheldon."[1]

In the month of April, 1632, the benefice of Ickford, a small village ten miles from Oxford, in the counties of Bucks and Oxon, became vacant, through the death of John Sellar, B.D., the rector. He was succeeded in the same year by a zealous Parliamentary advocate, named Calybute Downing, or, as he wrote his name in the Ickford Register, "Callybute Downinge." Later this man became chaplain to Lord Robartes' regiment in the Earl of Essex's army, and again (1643) licenser of books of divinity. In 1636 he resigned the benefice of Ickford to become rector of Hackney, a position he held until 1643 ; he died the next year.[2] Now, as we have seen, Gilbert Sheldon was instituted vicar of Hackney in May 1633, and evidently resigned the benefice in 1636-7. Thus, at Hackney, Sheldon was followed by Downing ; whilst at Ickford, Downing was followed by Sheldon. This is certainly a remarkable interchange, considering that the two men were poles apart in their convictions and sympathies—Sheldon being a staunch Churchman and Royalist, whilst Downing

---

[1] *The Works of William Chillingworth, M.A.*, Oxford, 1838, vol. i. pp. xxiv. xxviii.

[2] *Dict. Nat. Biog.*, sub. "Downing Calybute."

was a prominent Puritan and Parliamentarian. To make this somewhat confusing interchange of benefices clear, the following may be of use—

Ickford: Downing, 1632–6. Sheldon, 1636–60.

Hackney: Sheldon, 1633–7. Downing, 1637–43.

On the resignation of Calybute Downing, the patron of the benefice of Ickford being then a minor, the presentation lapsed to the Crown, and King Charles I preferred his chaplain, Gilbert Sheldon, to the vacancy. In a note, written in pencil in later times on the cover of the Ickford Register (A.D. 1561–1731), it is said that "Sheldon was presented to the Rectory of Ickford, May 8, 1636, vice Calibute Downing." Ignoring his rejection and the intrusion of some Puritan later, Sheldon legally held the benefice of Ickford until his preferment to the See of London in 1660. His successor at Ickford was Paul Hood, S.T.P., who was instituted rector in November 6, 1660. Sheldon was consecrated Bishop of London in October 28, 1660.

Sheldon's entries in the old Ickford Register commence July 10, 1636, and continue with great regularity year by year—but 4 entries out of 122, in another hand, excepted—until December 27,

1650. The following table shows the baptisms, marriages, and burials entered by Sheldon whilst rector of Ickford. In estimating the frequency of entries, it must be remembered that Ickford is but a small agricultural village—

THE ICKFORD REGISTER

Year.	Baptisms.	Marriages.	Burials.
1636–	6	0	0
1637–	8	1	3
1638–	2	2	2
1639–	9	2[1]	9
1640–	3	1	0
1641–	7	2	5
1642–	4	0	4
1643–	1[1]	0	0
1644–	3[2]	0	0
1645–	7	1	2
1646–	7	0	1
1647–	7	1	0
1648–	8	0	0
1649–	6	0	0
1650–	5	0	3
Total	83	10	29

In the collection of MSS. at the Salt Museum, Stafford, is preserved a bulky volume, containing

[1] Not Sheldon's handwriting.
[2] One, not Sheldon's handwriting.

the returns of a religious census taken by order
of Archbishop Sheldon in 1676. These returns
give the numbers of Conformists, Papists, and
Nonconformists, respectively, above the age of
sixteen. Ickford is there given as having 105
Conformists, 2 Papists, but no Nonconformists,
with an estimated entire population of 214.[1] This
would represent the population in Sheldon's time :
now it is about 330.

The entries of the years 1648, 1649, and 1650
possess a peculiar interest, as we shall now see :
they are reprinted in detail in Appendix III at
the close of this volume.

Dr. Fell, in his *Life of Dr. Hammond*, states
that—

"the reverend Dr. Sheldon, now lord bishop
of London, and dean of his Majesty's chapel
royal, and Dr. Hammond . . . by an order from
a committee of parliament were restrained and
voted to be prisoners in that place (Oxford),
from which all else were so severely driven."[2]

From Anthony à Wood, as we shall see in the
next chapter of this Life of Sheldon, we learn
that he was ejected from the wardenship of All
Souls College, Oxford, on April 13, 1648, and
presumably from the rectory of Ickford. From

---

[1] *Records of Bucks*, Aylesbury, 1899, pp. 146 ff.
[2] Fell, *Life of Dr. Hammond*, Oxford, 1856, pp. 135, 136.

the same source we learn that on the same day—

" Dr. Sheldon was sent forthwith to James Chesterman's house against the Cross Inn, with a guard of musketeers . . . and there was kept in safe custody till further pleasure." [1]

Sheldon was then imprisoned until October 24, 1648—

" In this durance he continued above six months, and then the Reforming Committee set him at liberty (October 24, 1648), after which he returned to his friends in Staffordshire and the adjoining counties." [2]

In the face of these statements, the evidence gathered from the parish register of St. Nicholas' Church, Ickford, is very perplexing, if not contradictory. Sheldon's entries commence in 1636; they are written in a small, yet beautifully clear and definitely characteristic style of handwriting. The entries for the three years 1648, 1649, 1650, are without any possibility of doubt in Sheldon's handwriting.

In the first place, it will be observed that during the time he was in close confinement, *i.e.* April 13 to October 24, 1648, there are three

---

[1] Wood's *Annals*, April 13, 1648; qu. later.

[2] Walker, *Sufferings of the Clergy* . . . Lond. 1714, Part II., p. 98.

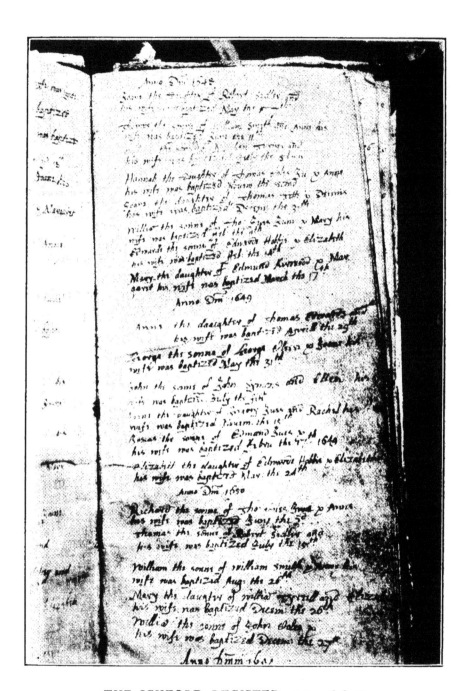

THE ICKFORD REGISTER, A.D. 1648-51

entries of his in the baptismal part of the register, viz., May 7, June 11, and July 5. How are we to account for these entries? Possibly the baptisms may have been performed by some other minister, and that Sheldon, having hidden or retained possession of the register, entered them himself later from notes given to him by the actual baptizer.

In the second place, the fourth entry of Baptisms, under 1648, is dated " Novem: the second "; that is, but nine days after his release from prison; whilst the next entry is under " Decem: the 31ᵗʰ." How are we to reconcile Sheldon's presence at Ickford (if he was the baptizer) with Walker's statement that, on regaining his liberty, " he returned to his friends in Staffordshire. . . ."? And what, too, is the explanation of the following entries of 1648, in February and March of that year, which suggest or imply Sheldon's presence at Ickford?

Moreover, a third difficulty presents itself, raised by the frequent entries in Sheldon's handwriting all through the next years, 1649 and 1650. The entries in these years bear the dates: A.D. 1649, April 29, May 31, July 1, November 15, February 17, and March 24; A.D. 1650, April 6, April 15, June 3, July 15, August 26, December 26,

December 27, February 26. A study of these dates in the years 1649, 1650, when the benefice of Ickford was presumably held by some intruded Puritan minister, shows that Sheldon must have been in residence, or at least a frequent visitor in his old, parish. Possibly he may have administered baptism in some Royalist house in the village or neighbourhood. But how are we to account for the three burials in 1650? The omission of burial entries in the two preceding years is very remarkable, also the omission of marriage entries in 1648, 1649, 1650. These omissions seem to point to some intruding Puritan minister being in possession of the benefice of Ickford, who had not access to the register. Probably Sheldon did not deliver it up, but kept it in his own possession; anyhow he had access to it.

There is a remarkable gap in the register for 1643 and 1644, for which it is difficult to account. In 1643 and 1644 Sheldon has entered "Anno Dñi 1643" and "Anno Dñi 1644" in the register of baptisms, leaving spaces of about five inches blank in the former year, whilst there follows but one entry of a baptism in another hand. In the latter year there is likewise a space of two inches occupied by but one entry in another hand. In the register of marriages there is a vacant space of four inches between September 26, 1641, and December 5, 1645. In the register of burials there is a space of more than three inches between February 18, 1642, and May 5, 1645. This hiatus has the appearance of being the period in which some Puritan intruder was in possession of the benefice of Ickford; but no direct evidence on the point is forthcoming. The absence of entries of marriages and burials in 1648 and 1649 is likewise perplexing, for it is improbable that for two years there were at least no deaths in a parish of a population of over 200 persons.

In 1651 the handwriting changes, and the register must have been in the custody of the Parliamentary minister. There is no evidence that Sheldon employed a curate at Ickford, as was the case when he was vicar of Hackney and rector of Newington.

There is another solution of the difficulty, suggested by the Ickford Register, which the present writer is inclined to think is the true one— namely, that whilst Sheldon was ejected from All Souls, Oxford, in 1648, his ejection from the benefice of Ickford did not take place until the end of December 1650. The process of ejection and intrusion throughout the land was slow and gradual, as we learn from Walker's *Sufferings of the Clergy*, which records Sheldon's ejection from All Souls, but is silent about Ickford. The County Committees appointed for ejecting the clergy were at work from 1643 all through the time of the Long Parliament. Again, where the lawful parish priests had been ejected, no intruding ministers were appointed in some cases for many years after, even as late as 1657 and 1661,[1] and it is possible that, in some of these cases clergymen, of such deep convictions and conspicuous courage as Gilbert Sheldon possessed, continued to minister though deprived of their incomes. Walker mentions an instance of a sequestration not taking place till as late as 1652 ;[2] and he tells us that Committees of Sequestration were sitting in the county of Devon from 1648 to 1653.[3] Sequestrations in Yorkshire were not taken in hand till 1649 ; whilst as late as 1653 (three years after Sheldon's entries at Ickford cease) "a project was on foot to send a new set of commissioners into the country to sequestrate the clergy. For this end the whole kingdom was to be divided into six circuits; to each of which 3 commissioners were to be sent from

---

[1] For the evidence of these long vacancies, see Walker, Part I., p. 97.
[2] *Ibid.*   [3] *Ibid.*, Part I., p. 87.

London, who were to be joined by 4 or 6 of each respective county within that circuit in which they should act."[1] In the following year (1654) an Act was passed appointing Commissioners to eject "scandalous, ignorant, and insufficient ministers."[2] As late as 1653 another sort of commissioners called "Tryers" were appointed, incidentally to harass and dispossess the lawful clergy; and there is evidence that these men were at work in the county of Devon, for example, soon after 1649 and also about 1651.[3]

In the face of this evidence, and taking the whole of the circumstances into consideration, it seems highly probable that Gilbert Sheldon retained possession of the benefice of Ickford— 1643 and part of 1644 perhaps excepted—until the close of December 1650, as suggested by the entries in the register of that parish.[4]

The parish church of St. Nicholas, Ickford, dating from the beginning of the thirteenth century, is a building of particular interest, and

[1] Walker, Part I., p. 170.   [2] *Ibid.*
[3] *Ibid.*, pp. 170, 171.
[4] Through the courtesy of the Rev. Henry Mare, vicar of Worminghall, half a mile distant from Ickford, I have been permitted to examine the register of the parish, and found that the legal parish priest returned to minister there in 1652. In three places in the register I find "Anno 1652, Francis Price, Vicar, *Existent.*" This signified that Price would not acknowledge the intending person as in legal possession.

is one of the most beautiful village churches in England.   After these pages were written, there appeared a handsome quarto volume, published under the auspices of the Royal Commission on Historical Monuments in England, dealing with South Buckinghamshire, and containing a detailed description of historical features existing in that county.[1]   In this work five columns are devoted to a minute description of Ickford Church, which is said to be " a church of especial interest, as it was built almost entirely in the thirteenth century, and retains much detail of that date." [2] Up to the beginning of the twentieth century, the chancel excepted, it had escaped so-called " restoration "; and, in consequence, happily retained features which otherwise would have been inevitably destroyed.   In 1906 a most careful and conservative restoration was commenced, under the guidance and direction of Mr. John Oldrid Scott.   The amount required to defray the cost of restoration (£1680) was subscribed mainly by the county of Bucks—there being no resident gentry in the parish at the time— under the direction of the late Cecil Bourke, Archdeacon of Bucks.   A brass tablet fixed to

[1] Published by His Majesty's Stationery Office, London, 1912.
[2] *Ibid.*, p. 214.

CHURCH OF ST. NICHOLAS, ICKFORD

a wall of the chancel, put up by the late Francis
Paget, Bishop of Oxford, records this good work.
It bears the following inscription, composed by
Dr. Paget just before his lamented death in the
summer of 1911 :—

1902–1911
In thankfulness for
the generosity and perseverance
of those who, under the guidance
of Cecil Bourke, Archdeacon of
Buckingham, undertook and carried
through the restoration of Ickford
Church, this tablet is set here
by Francis, Bishop of Oxford.

The successful restoration of the parish church
owed its accomplishment in some measure to the
desire to honour the memory of Gilbert Sheldon.
In the convocation held at Oxford on November
25, 1902, it was unanimously decreed—

"That the Curators of the Sheldonian Theatre
be authorised to contribute the sum of £50 to the
restoration of Ickford Church, Bucks, of which
Archbishop Sheldon was sometimes Rector . . .
its payment to be conditional upon the total sum
required (£1680) being collected, and the restoration carried out within two years from
January 1, 1903."

The curators made further grants later. The

church was reopened after restoration on Easter Even, March 30, 1907, by Dr. Paget, who preached from Isaiah lvi. 7: "I will make them joyful in my house of prayer."

The church consists of a chancel 26 feet long and 13 feet wide; a nave of the same width, 41 feet long, with narrow north and south aisles, 6 feet wide, of the same length as the nave; a western tower; and a south porch. At first sight the church has the appearance of being Transitional Norman, with a chancel of somewhat later date; not built all at one time, and the lower part of the tower may be Norman, while its upper storey is clearly later than the chancel. The differences in date are such as may be easily accounted for if the church were slowly rebuilt by degrees from an earlier structure. In the tower is an upper storey containing a pair of wide trefoil lights, each within a pointed arch, of the purest and most refined work of the thirteenth century. During the restoration an old stone *mensa* was discovered, used as a paving stone: it has been restored to its original use. On the north wall of the aisle, within a space of but 20 feet, are, side by side, a Norman doorway and window, an Early English lancet window, and a Decorated window. There are three drains

in the church and a holy water stoop; also an
aumbry for the reservation of the Eucharist.
The pulpit, a fine one, with a sounding-board,
and the pews are of oak of the seventeenth
century, possibly placed in the church by Sheldon.
There is, unfortunately, nothing in the church to
suggest any definite association with Sheldon
himself.

In 1897, before the restoration of the building,
Mr. W. H. St. John Hope, then assistant secretary of the Society of Antiquaries, visited Ickford
Church, and furnished a report on its condition
to the Society for the Protection of Ancient
Buildings, which was presented at its meeting
on March 18, 1897. In issuing the report, the
Society last named described the church as
"undeniably a work of art of particularly interesting and rather unusual character."[1] Before
leaving this subject it may be said that in the
chancel is a large and well-preserved Elizabethan
monument in memory of Thomas Tipping and
his wife Margaret, which has an inscription

---

[1] Mr. St. John Hope's report on Ickford Church is printed in
full in vol. vii., No. 6, of *Records of Buckinghamshire*, Aylesbury,
1897, pp. 550 ff. From this report the brief description above is
drawn. There is also a very accurate description of the church,
rectory, and village in the recently published *Inventory of the
Historical Monuments in Buckinghamshire*, vol. i., pp. 214-218,
with a fine picture of the church taken from the north-west.

redolent of the finest period of the English language, in two stanzas, the latter stanza reads :—

> " My soule and bodey be you fixt on christ youer strength and stay, he doth you keep he to himself recalleth you allway : contem ye torment and decease all worldly change despise, feare not the grave assuer youre selves with christ youer guide to rise : who shall prepare you princely seats youer lyght youer life youer crowne is he, rewarding all his saynts with glory and renowne."

The date of this monument is A.D. 1593, and thus the eyes of Gilbert Sheldon must oft have rested upon the magnificent diction of its inscription. Among the illustrations in this work are three of the Church of St. Nicholas, Ickford. In 1661, the year after Sheldon's advancement to the See of London, as a touching reminiscence of his love for his old village parish, its church and people, he presented a large and handsome silver communion cup and cover to Ickford, an illustration and description of which will be found elsewhere in the present volume. There are no traditions preserved in the village concerning him, we regret to say : his times were too remote for any to linger on. As he was

ST. NICHOLAS, ICKFORD

ST. NICHOLAS, ICKFORD

warden of All Souls, Oxford, at the same time
that he was rector of Ickford, he must have
driven to and fro[1], in order to fulfil his duties
at both places. Certainly, judging by the Ickford
registers, Sheldon did not neglect his village-
cure in favour of his high and important office
at the university.

In the same year that Sheldon was preferred
to the benefice of Ickford, King Charles I also
presented him to that of Oddington, near Islip.
He was instituted on July 19, 1636, and he
resigned the benefice in 1639, three years later,[2]
on his appointment to the rectory of Newington.
He was succeeded at Oddington by Thomas
Bourne on February 28, 1640–41. Of Sheldon's
work at this place nothing is forthcoming, though
inquiries have been made by the writer, and
courteously answered by the present rector.

On June 21, 1639, Gilbert Sheldon was instituted to the benefice of Newington, being presented thereto by Archbishop Laud,[3] and he held
this post legally until 1660, when he was preferred to the bishopric of London by King

[1] The high road to Oxford passes a mile and a half from
Ickford.

[2] Bishop's Certif., Oxon., F. Gm. 2.

[3] *Cant. Reg.*, Laud, 43.

Charles II. The earliest entries in Sheldon's handwriting in the register, which the present writer has examined, are in 1640—namely, a burial, July 10; a marriage, July 27; and a "christening," September 20. There are several of his entries in 1641, and a few others later. The majority of the entries are in another hand, evidently that of a curate resident at Newington. In Sheldon's absence "the duty" was carefully provided for. Under 1650 there is a very interesting note in the register—"Edward Archer Pastor by usurpation in ye rebellion agaynst King Charles the First. Dr. Sheldon being ye lawfull Rector." This is the year, at the close of which Sheldon's entries in the Ickford Register cease, and seems to mark the date of his ejection from both Newington and Ickford. In the midst of Pastor Archer's entries, and inserted between the lines at a later date, is the following entry in Sheldon's handwriting—"March 19, 1655, Anne Dormer the daughter of Willm Dormer of Ascott Gent., was baptized March 19, 1655. She was borne the 14 of March before." The Dormers of the time were a family of importance, and Sheldon evidently visited Newington during the intruded Pastor Archer's occupancy of the benefice, in order to baptize the five-day-old infant. Eventually he obtained possession of the register and entered the baptism between the lines. In regard to the first entries in Sheldon's hand at Newington, July 10, 27, and September 20, 1640, it is to be observed that there are entries in the Ickford Register in the same year on June 4, July 25, and August 14. Newington is by road about 9 miles from Ickford. After the evil custom of the times, Sheldon was a pluralist, holding simultaneously the wardenship of All Souls College, Oxford, and the benefices of Ickford, Oddington, and later of Newington. The revenues he derived from these positions must have been considerable, and account in some measure for his extraordinary munificence to private and public objects, of which more is to be said later; certainly he used the Church's goods for the Church's good. His liberality was unbounded and without parallel.

CHAPTER II

SHELDON, FELLOW AND WARDEN OF: ALL SOULS, OXFORD

Neglect of Sheldon's memory—His early connection with All Souls College, Oxford—Warden of All Souls—Courageous action in dealing with corrupt elections of Fellows—Opposition to Archbishop Laud—Denial of the Pope to be Anti-Christ—Jeremy Taylor elected Fellow of All Souls—Restoration of the Chapel of All Souls—Sheldon, a prominent adviser of King Charles I—Co-operation with Clarendon in the reorganisation of nation and Church—Commissioner at the Treaty of Uxbridge—Attended King Charles I at Oxford—The King sends for Sheldon to the Isle of Wight—High in the King's confidence—Charles the First's vow made before Sheldon—Disclosure of the vow to King Charles II—Bishop Duppa—William Juxon, Bishop of London—Burial of King Charles I at Windsor—Sheldon assists the ejected clergy—The Presbyterian ascendancy—Sufferings of the clergy—Sheldon with the King at Carisbrooke—Opposed to the Oxford Visitation—Ejection from the Wardenship of All Souls—William Prynne—Imprisonment of Sheldon—His release on conditions—Sends financial help to King Charles II—Restoration to Wardenship.

In speaking of Gilbert Sheldon, a modern writer has said—

"No man was more influential in promoting his views of Church and State within his University. No man was more fully in the confidence of Charles the First during the latter year of that monarch's life. No man had a greater share in keeping his party together during their adversity. No man exercised more authority than Sheldon in the re-settlement of affairs at the Restoration. Consequently no man's memory has been more bitterly attacked by the opponents of his principles. No man has been so successfully deprived of his just title to respect, if not to admiration. No man has been so completely deserted by modern writers of his own party. It may seem Quixotic to attempt to rehabilitate such a character, and to place it on the historic stage in any different light. It will certainly seem presumptuous."[1]

Such is the deliberate verdict of one—a Fellow of All Souls—after a thorough and careful study of the life and deeds of Gilbert Sheldon, both in the University of Oxford and out of it. And it is a verdict with which the present writer, after a similar and independent study of Sheldon's career, is in fullest accord. That Sheldon has been both misrepresented by his enemies and neglected by his friends is not open to dispute. As one of the greatest men in the Church of England of his day, this thing ought not to be. Simple justice, apart from

---

[1] Burrows, *Worthies of All Souls*, Lond., 1874, ix. 142.

compelling admiration and gratitude, alone de-
mands Sheldon's rehabilitation. We are not
acting in accordance with the injunction, " Let
us praise famous men,"[1] if we leave him out
of our reckoning. And yet, incredible as it is,
no public memorial has been set up in his
memory.

With these preliminary remarks we may proceed to attempt to describe Gilbert Sheldon's
connection with All Souls College, Oxford; and
we propose to devote this chapter to the task.

Sheldon became Fellow of All Souls in 1622;
thirteen years later he was elected Warden, that
is in 1635. We may deliberately regard him as
the most distinguished member of that college,
and consider his history both before and after
his expulsion from the wardenship as the history
of the college. Of the thirteen years of his
fellowship we have but slender information to
impart. During this time allusions are few, but
nevertheless suggestive of a character fearless
and independent. He showed courageous energy
in dealing with corrupt elections, and took a
strenuous part in oppressing them. In the first
year of Sheldon's wardenship, he steadily declined
to be forced to do a wrong, even by his close

[1] Ecclus. xliv 1.

ALL SOULS COLLEGE, OXFORD

From an old engraving

friend and patron, William Laud himself. The doctrine that was styled Arminianism had become popular and fashionable ; the King was a convert to it, and Laud was rising in influence; yet Sheldon opposed it. We may believe that his strong good sense was averse from either extreme adopted by the controversialists of the time, and led him to adopt the *via media* exhibited in the Articles.

From Kennett's Register we learn that Sheldon was "the first who publicly denied the Pope to be Anti-Christ," to the amazement of Dr. Prideaux, who was, during the disputation, 'Doctor of the Chair.' This was evidence of Sheldon's courage, in the face of the preface of the Authorised Version of the Holy Bible of 1611, which profanely identified the Bishop of Rome with "the Man of Sin."[1]

In 1633 Laud, as Archbishop of Canterbury, succeeded to the office of Visitor of All Souls, Oxford. One of the Fellows, Osborne by name, made over his Fellowship to the Archbishop, who recommended Jeremy Taylor (later Bishop of Connor and Down) for the vacancy. He was almost unanimously elected by the Fellows; but Sheldon, as Warden, exercised his veto

---

[1] James I is congratulated for " writing in the defence of the truth, which hath given such a blow unto that Man of Sin, and will not be healed."—*Preface to Holy Bible of* 1611.

with good reason. The Statutes of All Souls required that any candidate for a Fellowship must have three years standing as an Oxford student. Taylor could not claim this : he had indeed but ten days before the election been entered, by Laud's direction, by way of a colourable pretext, in the books of University College. Sheldon would have none of this, and rightly so. Laud had persuaded himself that there would be no difficulty in the matter ; and on the election devolving upon himself as Visitor, in consequence of the disagreement between the Warden and the Fellows of All Souls, he immediately appointed Jeremy Taylor to the vacant Fellowship. No doubt Laud, as Visitor, had an admirable end in view, and we might well be tempted to pass over such a splendid wrong as his intrusion of so great and able a man as Jeremy Taylor ; but there was a vital principle involved, and Gilbert Sheldon knew it, and strenuously opposed the high-handed proceeding as both unstatutable and unwarrantable. Laud's method of forcing his nominee upon the college in spite of all obstacles, was, sad to say, only too characteristic. His error was twofold—he refused to recognise the Statutes, and he had no authority to accept a vacancy at the hands of a resigning Fellow—

and we cannot excuse the action. Anthony à
Wood, who believed Jeremy Taylor to be under
age as well as a Cambridge man, condemned
Laud's action in the decided terms which it
deserved. Sheldon did the right thing, even
in resisting so great and good a man as his
friend, William Laud. It is an ungrateful task
to say a word to detract from the reverence
due to the Archbishop who laid down his life
for the Church, and who, by so doing, saved
the Church of England; but we gain nothing
by withholding the whole truth, but the reverse.
Bishop Heber, in his *Life of Jeremy Taylor*,
gives a full account of the incident, and he adds—

" The conduct of Sheldon throughout the affair
appears to have been at once spirited and conscientious; but it may have been marked by
some degree of personal harshness towards
Taylor, since we find that for some years after
a coolness subsisted between them, till the
generous conduct of the Warden produced a
sincere and lasting reconciliation." [1]

In the archives of All Souls are letters from
Laud which exhibit his care for the welfare of
the College. In one of these, written to Sheldon

[1] Heber, *Life of Jeremy Taylor*, *D.D.*, in "Jeremy Taylor's
Works," ed. Eden, vol. i. p. xix. Heber gives January 14, 1636,
as the date of Taylor's appointment at All Souls.

as Warden, complaint is made concerning the dress of the Fellows—

"This charge I require you, Mr. Warden, to deliver to all the Fellows, but especially the officers, that they use not long, undecent hair, nor wear large falling bands, nor boots under their gowns, nor any other like unstatutable novelty in their apparel."

This letter is signed, "Your very loving friend and Visitor, W. Cant." [1]

It was during Sheldon's Fellowship that we first hear of some attempt to restore the Chapel of All Souls, "the Chantry of peculiar magnificence," to decency and order, after its violation and disfigurement at the hands of the commissioners of the reign of Edward VI. The numerous altars, the many statues which adorned the splendid reredos, left a mere wreck of its original magnificence, had been destroyed or mutilated; the altar which was retained had been removed from its old place. As early as 1619 we find mention of a " murrey velvet carpet with gold and silk fringe for the Communion Table"; but in 1629, when Laud's influence was supreme, but before he became Visitor, we read that "the Communion Table was advanced from ye midle of the Chancell

---

[1] Burrows, *Worthies of All Souls*, p. 148.

to yᵉ upper end above the ascending steps."
When Sheldon became Warden in 1635, the
beginnings of restoration are discerned, and some
necessary repairs made, but the ruined reredos,
for which All Souls Chapel is famous, was not
touched at this time. There still exists a subscription book with an entry by Sheldon recording his disbursement of £200 on repairs. We
hear no more of this matter of restoring the
Chapel for a generation.

"The blindest must have perceived that the
storm which had so long been lowering over the
land was about to break in all its fury. To spend
money upon Chapels was indeed to throw it away.
We may well imagine with what reluctance such
men as Sheldon, Jeremy Taylor, and Duck, supported no doubt by Laud, Duppa, and Steward,
would give up their darling scheme." [1]

The time had at length arrived when Gilbert
Sheldon was called upon to stand forth prominently as one of King Charles the First's chief advisers, and to take his place amongst the eminent
and leading political and ecclesiastical men in England. And, as such, his influence increased until,
at the Restoration, he had attained to a position
scarcely second to that held by Lord Clarendon.

[1] Burrows, p. 152.

It was by these two fast friends that both Church and State were re-established on that firm basis which has endured for two and a half centuries.

During the Great Rebellion and the Commonwealth, Sheldon adhered loyally to the royal cause, and in 1644 he was, as the King's chaplain, sent by his Majesty Charles I to attend his commissioners at the Treaty of Uxbridge, where he spoke so earnestly and argued so effectively in favour of the Church, that he incurred the hostility of the Parliamentary commissioners; later they gave him a decided proof of their resentment by ejecting him from his post of Warden of All Souls College, Oxford, to which he was elected in 1635.

In the month of April, 1646, Sheldon attended Charles I, as his Chaplain and Clerk of the Closet, at Oxford, where he witnessed a remarkable vow made by the King, to which reference will be made later. In 1647 some letters passed between Sheldon and several gentlemen who were imprisoned in the Tower of London for the royal cause, and who had scruples in applying to the usurping authorities for their liberty. They feared that, by so doing, they might prejudice the King's interest and prospects. The matter was submitted to his Majesty, who bade them use their own judgment and act as they felt best. During the King's visit to Newmarket in the same year, and later in the Isle of Wight, Sheldon attended him as one of his chaplains.

The misfortunes and lamentable end of Charles I have been attributed by Daniel Neal, the Puritan historian, to the mistaken counsels of the divines his Majesty took into his confidence, and who would not permit him to make such concessions to the Puritan party in regard to the Church as would have saved his life. Of these advisers Sheldon was undoubtedly the most important. He rendered to the King powerful assistance at the time of the negotiations with the Parliament at Uxbridge, as already stated. In 1647, when his Majesty was a prisoner in the Isle of Wight, he sent for Sheldon, who, aided by Hammond, Morley, and Stevenson, discussed the demands of Parliament, and suggested to him how far he could in good conscience concede to these de-mands. And, as I have elsewhere said, Sheldon was kept in close confinement after his expulsion from All Souls, at Oxford, lest he should again go to the assistance of his royal master, who was now imploring permission for his attendance.

That Sheldon was the man who most enjoyed the King's confidence, who was in fact his chief friend and most trusted adviser, is evident from the following remarkable transaction of which we will now speak.

In April 1646 Charles the First was in Oxford for the last time. Shortly before his last farewell to the city and university he made a vow, recorded in writing, and signed by his own hand. This vow he entrusted to Gilbert Sheldon for its safe keeping, until the time should happily arrive for its fulfilment. Alas! that time never came: the King was beheaded at Whitehall within two years from the date of the vow. The vow was buried underground by Sheldon for thirteen years, and reproduced by him with his signature of attestation in 1660. It is quite extraordinary that no historian of first-class note has even referred to it, important as it is in more directions than one. It was left to Laurence Echard,[1] who became

---

[1] As shedding some light on Echard's source of information as to the vow of Charles I, it is to be observed that Anthony à Wood relates, that on a certain occasion, in the year 1671, he was at Lambeth, where " Archbishop Sheldon received him and gave him his blessing " ; and that among the company at dinner was one " Joh. Echard, the author of *The Contempt of the Clergy*, who sate at the Lower end of the Table between the Archbishop's two Chaplays Sam. Parker and Tho. Thomkins, being the first time that the said Echard was introduced into the said Archbishop's company." — *Lives of John Leland, Thomas Hearne, and Anthony à Wood*, Oxford, 1772, vol. ii. p. 247. To this John Echard, Laurence Echard, who records the vow, was closely related. See Chalmers, *Biograph. Dict.*, sub. " Laurence Echard."

Archdeacon of Stowe in 1712, to publish to the world, in 1718, in the Appendix to his *History of England*, the vow of Charles I. Le Neve, in his *Lives of the Bishops*, shortly after the publication of Echard's *History*, also gave the vow in full. Whilst in the *Clarendon State Papers* (2176 Bodleian Library) the authentic copy which Echard quoted is still to be seen. In 1816 Alexander Chalmers, F.S.A., published a new and revised edition of his useful *General Biographical Dictionary*, and, under " Sheldon,"[1] he wrote—

" In April, 1646, Sheldon attended the King at Oxford, and was witness to a remarkable vow which his majesty made there, the purport of which was, that when it should please God to re-establish his throne, he would restore to the Church all impropriations, lands, &c., which were taken from any episcopal see, cathedral, collegiate church, &c. This vow, which is in the appendix to Echard's history, was preserved thirteen years under ground by Dr. Sheldon."

Mr. Montagu Burrows' attention was drawn to the King's vow, independently of Chalmers' reference, by the discovery of a MS. letter of Brian Duppa (Bishop of Salisbury) of 1660, which he found in the Bodleian Library, Oxford, in

[1] Vol. xxvii. p. 443. As to whether this passage appeared in the earlier edition of Chalmers' *Biog. Dict.* the present writer does not know.

which certain "buried papers" are named. This letter of Duppa is quoted later in this volume.

The vow of King Charles I is here reproduced *verbatim et literatim.*

The Vow.

"I doe here promise and solemnly vow, in the presence and for the service of Almighty God, that if it shall please his Divine Matie of his infinite goodness to restore me to my just kingly rights, and to re-establish mee in my throne, I will wholly give back to his Church all those Impropriations whᶜʰ are now held by the Crowne; and what lands soever I now doe or shall enjoy which have been taken away either from any Episcopall See or any Cathedrall or Collegiate Church, from any Abbey or other Religious House. I likewise promise for hereafter to hold them from the Church under such reasonable Fines and Rents as shall be set downe by some conscientious persons, whome I promise to choose wᵗʰ all uprightnes of Heart to direct me in this particular. And I most humbly beseech God to accept of this my Vow, and to blesse me in the designes I have now in hand, through Jesus Christ our Lord. Amen.

"Charles R.

"Oxford, the 13th *April,* 1646."

" This is a true copye of the King's Vow wch was preserved thirteene yeares under ground by mee.   GILBERT SHELDON.

"*Aug.* 21st 1660."

The disclosure of this document to King Charles II in 1660 had doubtless a great effect upon the course he took at one of the most critical and momentous periods of the life of the English nation.   It certainly serves to pour some light upon the character of the Royal Martyr. It has been well said that—

"Charles the First is by no means a faultless prince.   There are transactions of which we can only say that a high-minded man seems to have been misled by the mischievous casuistry of the times ; but if one who preferred to run any risk rather than sacrifice his Church—and with all deductions it comes to that at last—deserves the name of martyr, that sacred name ought scarcely to be denied him, as it so often is by modern writers ; nor will the impression of his just right to the title be weakened by discovering that he had bound himself in the most solemn manner before a competent witness to perform, if he survived, an act of justice to the Church which no one else, it need hardly be said, has shewn any signs of even meditating." [1]

[1] Burrows, *Worthies of All Souls*, Lond., 1874, p. 180.

It is pathetic to know that the King's vow is dated just fourteen days before Charles I "early in the morning went out of Oxford, attended only by John Ashburnham and a Divine (one Hudson), who understood the byways as well as the common, and was indeed a very skilful guide,"[1] on his fatal journey to Scotland. How readily can we picture the scene and circumstances under which the unhappy King, well-nigh hunted to death by his foes, set his honoured name to the vow of reparation. But three weeks later Charles I was a prisoner in the Scottish camp, within the net from which was no escape. His doom was sealed.

But, to continue the history of the King's vow. In the Tanner MSS., vol. xlix. fol. 17, is found a letter from Dr. Duppa, Bishop of Salisbury, dated August 11 (1660), addressed: "For the Dean of His Majesty's Chapel"—that is, for Sheldon, upon whom the appointment was bestowed by King Charles II when they met at Canterbury, most probably on the suggestion of Hyde, later Lord Clarendon, who naturally wished to have Sheldon near at hand, to assist him in the arduous task which awaited him. After expressing his grave anxiety as to the state of

---

[1] Clarendon, *History of the Rebellion*, vol. iii. p. 22.

affairs, and his powerlessness to help effectively, through the pressure of old age, Duppa writes to Sheldon thus—

"You are the only person about His Majesty that I have confidence in, and I persuade myself that as none hath his ear more, so none is likely to prevail on his heart more, and there was never more need of it; for all the professed enemies of our Church look upon this as the critical time to use their dernier resort to shake His Majesty's constancy. But I hope by this time you have recovered those buried papers which can't but have a powerful influence upon so dutiful a soul as his. I shall wait upon you so soon as I hear that my coming may be any way useful. In the mean time I am the more at ease because I know you stand ready upon the place to lay hold upon all opportunities, and are diligently upon your watch *ne ecclesia aliquid detrimenti capiat.* For which, and for all your kindness to me in particular, I am your most affectionate friend,

"BR. SARUM."

It is not open to doubt that the King's vow was one of the "buried papers" referred to by Duppa in his letter of August 11. Ten days later, "August 21st, 1660," Gilbert Sheldon added his signature to the vow, and witnessed thereby that it was "a true copye of the King's Vow which was preserved thirteene yeares under ground by mee." Evidently he had just recovered the document at the suggestion of Duppa, to use it to some purpose with Charles II. A considerable length of time had elapsed since the restoration of the King, and yet he had strangely delayed to fill up the vacant sees. In the eyes of Sheldon and others the delay was disastrous. What took place between the King and the Dean of the Chapel we cannot say; but, within a fortnight of the date upon which Sheldon had attached his signature to the recovered vow, the King began to set about the filling of the vacant sees. The *congé d'élire* for Juxon to the primacy was issued on September 3; Duppa was translated to Winchester seven days later; whilst, on September 28, Gilbert Sheldon was himself recommended by the King for the see of London. The other vacant bishoprics were soon filled. It is difficult not to connect the production of the vow of Charles I by Sheldon with these events.

Later in this chapter I will attempt to trace Sheldon's career up to the eve of the overthrow of the King and the Church, at the outbreak of the Great Rebellion. Charles I, Gilbert Sheldon's first royal patron, was beheaded at Whitehall on January 30, 1649, and henceforward, for thirteen years, a new order of things was to prevail in both Church and State.

William Juxon, Bishop of London, whom Gilbert Sheldon succeeded in that see, and with whom he was later destined to be so closely connected, was called upon to perform the solemn duty of ministering to King Charles I on the scaffold at Whitehall on that fatal day, January 30, 1649. Juxon, passionately loved by the loyal for this act of fidelity, took his place at the head of the vault in St. George's Chapel, Windsor,[1] with his Book of Common Prayer spread open to begin the burial service, just eight days later, only to be forbidden by Colonel Whichcote, Governor of the Castle. Juxon had so far conciliated his enemies during his prosperity, that, obnoxious to none, he was permitted for a short

---

[1] Under the influence of Oliver Cromwell the ruling authorities consented to the decent burial of the Royal Martyr, and it was wisely determined that his body should be laid unostentatiously in a grave prepared for it in St. George's Chapel, Windsor. "The Bishop of London, together with the noblemen and gentlemen, to whom the performance of the royal obsequies was entrusted, proceeded, meanwhile, to select a proper resting-place for his remains. This was necessary, because the interior of the building, spoiled by the superstition or mistaken piety of the Puritans, lay in a state of melancholy devastation. As they searched, they came upon the graves of King Henry VIII and of Queen Jane Seymour, and here they determined to lay their late royal master. The body of King Charles, it was decided, should lie in this vault over against the eleventh stall of the sovereign's side of the choir. On the

time to retire to Fulham. Later, he made his home on his estate at Little Compton, Gloucestershire. He appears to have had some private means, and to have been in comfortable circumstances. Whilst he assisted several of the ejected clergy, there is no record that, like Gilbert Sheldon and other loyalists, he sent money to the Court of King Charles II. Possibly this may account for the fact that the Puritans left him in peace, though he seems to have lived in some fear of persecution, for in his house there was a hole in the wall wherein, in case of emergency, he could hide. In the face of the severe penalties attached to the use of the Book of Common Prayer, every Sunday, at the house of a family of the name of Jones, Juxon bravely performed the service, many of the inhabitants of Little Compton attending.

During the presbyterian ascendancy the clergy

7th February the royal remains were carried from the king's bedchamber into St. George's Hall, and thence they were borne to the chapel. The day had been fine when the little procession started, but before it entered the chapel the snow had fallen so quickly that the velvet pall was perfectly white, and those who stood around the grave were trembling with cold. . . . The coffin was lowered; the mourners looked in upon the grave; and there, on a silver plate attached to its leaden surface, the mourners read the simple inscription, 'King Charles, 1648.' Over the coffin was thrown the black pall by which it had been previously covered."— Hook, *Lives of the Archbishops of Canterbury*, London, 1875, vol. xi. pp. 415, 416.

REREDOS OF ALL SOULS CHAPEL, OXFORD

of the Church of England had endured terrible
sufferings. Clergymen, pious and venerable in
years, were driven from their parishes and imprisoned; and, as though to add insult to injury,
were prosecuted as absentees. The deprived
clergy and their families were reduced to starva-
tion and destitution. Some show of providing
for their barest needs had, it is true, been made
by an ordinance which required that one-fifth
part of the revenue of each benefice should be
paid to the family of the deprived parish priest.
But even this miserable pittance was not infrequently withheld by the intruding presbyterian
minister, or evaded by prosecuting the ejected
clergyman for absence from his parish—an act
of hypocrisy simply damnable in its insincerity.[1]
For the evidence here we have but to consult
John Walker's "Attempt towards recovering an
Account of the Number and Sufferings of the
Clergy of the Church of England, Heads of
Colleges, Fellows, Scholars, &c., who were
Sequester'd, Harrass'd, &c., in the late Times of
the Grand Rebellion."[2] Gilbert Sheldon, as a
prominent loyalist, in close attendance upon the
King, was marked out for attack. He had been

---

[1] See Hook, *Lives of the Archbishops of Canterbury*, xi. 418.
[2] Lond., 1714; the date of the publication of the first edition.

D

with Charles at Carisbrooke when the Parliamentary Visitors commenced their work of persecution; but he was at his post in Oxford when the final measures were adopted and the ejections were taken in hand. As a steadfast adherent to the royal cause, when the Oxford Visitation came on, he openly and strenuously opposed it. Was it likely that he should flinch from the struggle, just returned fresh from the side of his doomed master and friend? On March 27, 1648, the Visitors had confronted him at Oxford, and he boldly told them to their faces that " he could not with a safe conscience submit to them." [1] This is quite consistent with Sheldon's courage. But three days later Sheldon was deprived of his office of Warden of All Souls, Oxford, and a certain John Palmer, a " Bachelour of Physick," was substituted in his place and position. This was done contrary to the statutes of the college. [2] On April 3, the same year, the notice of Sheldon's expulsion was affixed to his lodgings at All Souls,

[1] The reader is referred to Appendix II., at the close of this volume, for Walker's account of the transaction, transcribed from his *Sufferings of the Clergy*.

[2] See Wood, *Athenæ Oxonienses*, i. 397. From Wood's *Annals*, A.D. 1648, we learn that " Dr. Sheldon was sent forthwith to James Chesterman's house against the Cross Inn, with a guard of musqueteers followed by a great company of scholars, and blessed by the people as he passed the streets, and there was kept in safe custody till further pleasure."

and at the same time Palmer's election was published. Ten days later the Visitors, with the Earl of Pembroke at their head, visited All Souls College, in order to dispossess and expel Sheldon by force, and intrude their nominee in his place. Sheldon, evidently in great straits, expostulated with the Visitors, pleading that their commission did not reach him, because it was dated March 8 ; that is, three weeks before the authorities had voted him out of possession. This plea of dis- crepancy of dates cost the Visitors an hour's debate ; but at last the notorious Prynne,[1] who was one of them, cut the knot, declaring that Sheldon, though outside the letter of the commis- sion, was nevertheless within the equity of it, and that he must not be suffered to make sport of the Parliament. Accordingly they proceeded to

[1] It must have called up all Sheldon's fortitude to find himself confronted by William Prynne, the notorious lawyer of the time, whose book *Histriomastix*, which came out in 1632, had given such offence at Court, and who in the next year was sentenced by the Star Chamber to be fined £5000 to the King, expelled the University of Oxford and Lincoln's Inn, to stand in the pillory and lose his ears, and be branded with a hot iron on his cheeks as a "Seditious Libeller," to have his offending book publicly burnt before his face, and to remain a prisoner for life. This inexpres- sibly cruel and barbarous treatment of Prynne had a great deal to do with bringing on the Civil War and the overthrow of Crown and Church. No wonder Prynne became the relentless, merciless foe of Church and King.

Prynne had been sentenced along with Bastwicke and Burton. The account of the trial is given in the *Harleian Miscellany*, vol. iv. pp. 16 ff. "*The Lord* Cottington's *Censure*—I Condemn these

deprive him of his freehold, striking his name out of the Buttery-book, and substituting Palmer's name in his stead. Further, they put Sheldon in custody, the Earl of Pembroke alleging as a reason that he had failed or refused to open the great gate when the Earl arrived. The Visitors then proceeded to violence, forcing open the doors of Sheldon's rooms, putting the intruder in possession, and hurrying Sheldon away to prison, first in Oxford with Dr. Hammond, Sub-Dean of Christchurch, and then in other places. We are told that as Dr. Sheldon passed along the streets of Oxford, he had "a thousand prayers and blessings from the people."[1] No doubt Sheldon's extraordinary liberality had made him to be much loved in Oxford. The following is a copy of the document ordering his arrest—

---

three Men to lose their Ears in this Palace-Yard at *Westminster;* to be fined Five-thousand Pounds a Man to his Majesty : And to perpetual Imprisonment in three remote Places of the Kingdom, namely, the Castles of *Caernarvon, Cornwall,* and *Lancaster. The Lord* Finch *added to this Censure*—Mr. *Prynne* to be stigmatised in the Cheeks with two Letters (S and L) for a seditious Libeller. To which all the Lords agreed. And so the *Lord Keeper* concluded the Censure." This diabolical sentence was carried out to the letter on June 30, 1637, with the additional severity of exposition at the Pillory.—*Ibid.*, pp. 21 ff.

Anthony à Wood, in his *Athenæ Oxon.*, iii. 847, states that in April, 1634, William Prynne "was solemnly degraded in the University of Oxon. and his name dashed out of the *Matricula.*"

[1] Wood, *Athen. Oxon.*, i. 403 ; Walker, *Sufferings, &c.*, ii. 98.

An order for commitment of Dr. Sheldon for refusing to submitt to the authority of the Visitors of the Universitie of Oxon.

WHEREAS Dr. Gilbert Sheldon, late Warden of All Souls Coll. in the University of Oxford, being several tymes summoned to appeare before us appoynted Visitors of the said Universitie by several Ordinances of Parliament and a Commission under the Great Seale of England, hath contemptuously refused to submitt to the authority conferred upon us by the said Ordinances and Commission, and obstinately denyed to deliver up the Statutes and Register Book as also the Warden's Lodgings of the said College, according to the contents of an order of the Committee of Lords and Commons for regulating the said University, being dated the 30th of March last, for the establishing of Mr. Jo. Palmer, Bach. of Physicke, Warden of the said College, to enjoy and have all the power, rights, emoluments, roomes and lodgings, by any Statute, Custome or Right belonging to the Warden thereof: These are therefore to will and require you by vertue of the said Ordinances and Commission to take into yor custodie the bodie of the said Dr. Gilbert Sheldon for his said contempt, and him saffely to keepe till hee shall be delivered by order of law. Whereof you are not to faile as you shall **answere** the contrary, and for yor soe doing this shall be yor Warrant.[1]

The Report of these proceedings was read in the House of Lords on April 21, and it contains the words, " Dr. Sheldon, the former Warden of All Souls, was committed for his contemptuous carriage." [2]

Sheldon was confined in prison for the space of six months, during which an attempt was made to secure his removal to Wallingford Castle, on the ground that his continuance in prison was dangerous from the fact that a large number of persons resorted to him. This attempt failed, the governor of the castle refusing to receive him. This is related by Dr. Fell, Dean of Christ Church, a contemporary with Dr. Sheldon at Oxford, in his *Life of Hammond*, who says—

" The officer who was commanded to take Dr. Sheldon and Dr. Hammond into custody, upon their designed removal, colonel Evelin, then governor of Wallingford castle (though a man of as opposite principles to church and

---

[1] *The Acts of the Visitation of Oxford Universitie; by Commissioners authorised by ye Long Parliament* (known as MS. e Musaeo 77.), p. 15. This MS. is in the Bodleian Library.

[2] *Journal of the House of Lords*, vol. x. p. 216,

churchmen as any of the adverse party), wholly declined the employment ; solemnly protesting, that if they came to him, they should be entertained as friends, and not as prisoners." [1]

On September 28, 1648, the Visitors approached Sheldon, and inquired where he intended to reside. He so far satisfied them, that on October 24, 1648, the Reforming Committee gave him his liberty on certain conditions, namely, (1) that he should at once remove himself five miles from Oxford ; (2) that he should not visit the King in the Isle of Wight ; [2] (3) that he should give security to appear before the Committee at four days' notice whensoever cited. [3] Mr. Richard Newdigate, of Gray's Inn, became Sheldon's security. Upon his release, it is said, he went to Snelston in Derbyshire, where he had friends. [4] There is, however, indisputable evidence, which has been given in the last chapter, that Sheldon was at Ickford from May 7, 1648 to December

---

[1] Fell, *Life of the Rev. H. Hammond*, Oxon, 1856, p. 136.
[2] The King was at the time imprisoned at Carisbrooke, and begging that Sheldon might be allowed to visit him there.
[3] Wood, *Athen. Oxon.*, i. 413.
[4] Walker says that Sheldon went to Staffordshire, but the entries in the Parish Register of Ickford unmistakably show that Sheldon was at Ickford, ten miles from Oxford, on November 2, 1648, eight days after his release.

27, 1650—at least he appears to have been there very frequently.

King Charles I was beheaded on January 30, 1649. His son and successor to the crown was in exile in France. Sheldon's loyalty to the throne remained as firm as ever. From his own private means, aided by contributions collected from his friends, he constantly sent large sums of money to the exiled King. On the Restoration in 1660 Charles II did not forget Sheldon's loyalty, his sufferings for the royal cause, and his generosity, as we shall see later.

The events we have just recalled to memory are briefly yet significantly described in the Records of All Souls College at the Restoration —" 1648; Pulso per vim Doctore Sheldon, Joannes Palmer, Med. Dr. a Parliamento Pseudo-Custos constituitur."

On March 4, 1659, John Palmer, " Pseudo-Custos," the intruder upon Sheldon's post at All Souls, died, and as there was some immediate prospect of the return of the King, and the restoration of the Church, no successor was elected to the wardenship. Thereupon Sheldon resumed his position at All Souls, though he did not appear in person to repossess himself of his rights and privileges: he was called upon at

once to assist Clarendon and Charles II in the re-settlement of the Church and nation; and it may safely be asserted that no Ministers during the whole course of English history had before them a more difficult task than that which fell to the lot of Clarendon and Sheldon. And who shall refuse them their due amount of honour in the way they carried that task through? As we survey the complicated situation, the character of the facile King who had hampered them with conditions and promises, and so tied their hands, his unworthy courtiers with whom they had to reckon, the balance of conflicting interests to be reconciled—as we try to put our minds back to the time of the Restoration, the words spoken to Queen Esther by Mordecai do not seem inappropriate in their significance in the case of both Clarendon and Sheldon—" Who knoweth whether thou art not come to the kingdom for such a time as this ? " [1]

Before closing this chapter, dealing with Gilbert Sheldon's connection with All Souls, it is to be observed that from 1635, when he was elected Warden, until 1677, when he passed to his rest, he was engaged in perpetual conflict with the Court on the one hand, and the Fellows of the

[1] Esther iv. 14.

College on the other, to secure that freedom of elections which Archbishop Chicheley, the founder, had appointed. And he did not strive in vain. Through Sheldon's strenuous efforts the cause was won, and the abuse ceased.

PART II

SHELDON AFTER THE RESTORATION

CHAPTER III

SHELDON, BISHOP OF LONDON—THE SAVOY CONFERENCE—LEGISLATION AGAINST THE PURITANS

The Declaration of Breda—Return of King Charles II—Enthusiasm of the Nation—John Evelyn's description of Charles II's entry into London—Primacy of Juxon—Sheldon advanced to the See of London—Lord Falkland's prophecy—Coronation of King Charles II—Charles II and the Presbyterians—Restoration of the Book of Common Prayer—The Savoy Conference and Sheldon's presidency thereat—Failure of the Savoy Conference—Legislation hostile to the Puritans—Passing of the Act of Uniformity—Lord Clarendon's account of the attitude of the Puritans—"Black Bartholomew," 1662—Animosity towards the Church party—Historical review of the situation—Further measures taken against the Puritans—The Conventicle Act—The Five Mile Act—Decrease of Nonconformity—Sheldon's action against delay in dealing with the Puritan ministers—Sheldon as a divine—His printed remains.

In 1660 King Charles II, in the Declaration of Breda, promised a general pardon, religious toleration, and satisfaction to the army. This declaration was received by a great burst of national enthusiasm. The old constitution was restored by a solemn vote of the Convention;[1] both Houses of Parliament instantly invited the King to return to his country and his throne. Hardly had this vote been passed, when King Charles landed at Dover, and proceeded, amidst a wild scene of excited congratulation, to Whitehall. " The world of England was perfectly mad," says Anthony à Wood in his Diary, "'It is my own fault,' laughed the new King, with characteristic irony, 'that I had not come back sooner; for I find nobody who does not tell me he has not always longed for my return.'"[2] The entry of King Charles II into Whitehall on May 29, 1660, is an event of greatest importance. It not only signified the restoration of the Crown, but also that of the Church. And we can well, in its light, understand the significance of the entries in the Book of Common Prayer of A.D. 1661–2 in the Kalendar, " January 30, King Charles Martyr," and " May 29, King Charles II Nativity and Restoration," and the additions, made in that edition of the Prayer Book to the Tables of Feasts and Fasts, of " The Thirtieth Day of

[1] " The Convention " is the term used to describe accurately the new Parliament of 1660, which was, of necessity, called without the royal writ, the King being abroad.

[2] Green, *Short Hist. of the English People*, Lond., 1874, p. 582. For a glowing account of the joy of the nation at the return of the King, see Macaulay's *Hist. of England*, Lond., 1849, i. 150.

January, being the Day kept in Memory of the Martyrdom of King Charles the First," and " The Nine and Twentieth Day of May, being the Day kept in Memory of the Birth and Return of King Charles the Second."[1]   And it is, moreover, not without interest in this memoir of Gilbert Sheldon to observe that these additions to the Book of Common Prayer were made at the last revision of that Book by the Convocation, over whose deliberations Sheldon presided.   But more of this later in this biography.

John Evelyn, an eye-witness, records in his *Diary*, under May 29, 1660—

" This day, his Majesty Charles the Second came to London, after a sad and long exile and calamitous suffering both of the King and Church, being seventeen years.   This was also his birthday, and with a triumph of above 20,000 horse and foot, brandishing their swords, and shouting, with inexpressible joy ; the ways strewed with flowers, the bells ringing, the streets hung with tapestry, fountains running with wine ; the Mayor, Aldermen, and all the Companies, in their liveries, chains of gold, and banners ; Lords and Nobles, clad in cloth of silver, gold, and velvet ; the

---

[1] These additions have been illegally omitted in modern editions of the Book of Common Prayer without authority.   Against this omission Churchmen have every right loudly to protest.

windows and balconies, all set with ladies; trumpets, music, and myriads of people flocking, even so far as from Rochester, so as they were seven hours in passing the city, even from two in the afternoon till nine at night. I stood in the Strand, and beheld it, and blessed God. And all this was due without one drop of blood shed, and by that very army which rebelled against Him."[1]

The Restoration of Church and Crown in 1660 found Juxon, the Bishop of London, a man close upon eighty years of age,[2] suffering from a distressing and incurable complaint. No doubt he shared in the exuberant delight with which the return of the King, significant of the restoration of peace, law, and freedom, was hailed throughout the length and breadth of the land; for the vast majority of the nation had remained loyal to their monarch. Though advanced in years and very infirm, Juxon's mind was unimpaired; and it would not have been tolerated that the ecclesiastic, who had stood by the first Charles and comforted him in his supreme moment of martyrdom, should not have been chosen to anoint and crown his successor in the throne of England.

[1] *Diary and Correspondence of John Evelyn*, Lond., 1850, vol. i. p. 337.
[2] Juxon was born A.D. 1582.

The See of Canterbury was vacant by the martyr-dom of Archbishop Laud in 1645. There were many good reasons why Sheldon might have been called to the primacy, but he was far - seeing enough to desire to stand aside and make way for Juxon, whose appointment afforded wide-spread satisfaction. On September 13, 1660, Bishop Juxon was elected to the primacy, and his confirmation took place seven days later. Juxon's translation to Canterbury left the See of London vacant; it was immediately filled by the consecration of Gilbert Sheldon in Henry VII's Chapel, Westminster, on October 28, being the Feast of St. Simon and St. Jude, 1660, by the Bishop of Winchester, assisted by the Bishops of Ely, Rochester, and Chichester, and the Arch-bishop of York. Morley and Sanderson were also consecrated to the episcopate on the same occasion, under a commission issued by Arch-bishop Juxon. As step by step William Juxon had followed William Laud—as Fellow, then as President of St. John's College, as Bishop of London, and eventually as Primate—so Sheldon followed Juxon as Bishop of London and then as Archbishop of Canterbury. Sheldon's promotion to the See of the capital thus took place five months after he had met the King on his return

E

at Canterbury, and in the interval he had been appointed Dean of the Chapel Royal, known as the Savoy. Sheldon held the mastership of the Savoy together with the bishopric of London. It had been the intention of Charles I that Sheldon, his chaplain-in-ordinary, should fill the former post; but the commotion and confusion of the time hindered the realisation of this intention. The action of the Royal Martyr's son, at the Restoration, in this matter was a graceful recognition of his father's wishes, not to be passed over unnoticed. It was whilst Sheldon was still a Fellow of All Souls that Lord Clarendon drew his picture in his happiest manner. In that famous account of Lord Falkland's house at Great Tew, amongst a brilliant company there wont to assemble, we find the name of " Dr. Sheldon" standing first. And, in another well-known passage, Clarendon speaks of

" Dr. Sheldon's learning, gravity, and prudence in that time, and when he was afterwards Warden of all Souls College in Oxford, which raised him to such a reputation that he then was looked upon as very equal to any preferment the Church could yield or hath since yielded to him; and Sir Francis Wenman would often say, when the Doctor resorted to the conversation at Lord

Falkland's house, as he frequently did, that Dr. Sheldon was born and bred to be Archbishop of Canterbury."[1]

This prediction was fulfilled later, as we shall see.

To return to Archbishop Juxon—the ceremonies surrounding the coronation of King Charles II on April 22–24, 1661, as we learn from Clarendon and Evelyn,[2] were carried out on an extraordinarily magnificent scale. The procession from the Tower of London to Whitehall on April 22 was of the character of a great ovation; and the ceremonial splendours were repeated on the following day, April 23, when his Majesty proceeded from Whitehall to Westminster for his sacring. He was received at the Abbey Church of St. Peter by the bishops vested in copes, and other ecclesiastics of note. Archbishop Juxon was too ill and infirm to take part in the procession, nevertheless the anointing and the coronation were performed by his hands. With the exception of the presentation of the King to the people, by Sheldon, at the four sides of the daïs on which the coronation chair was placed, the aged Archbishop performed his part

[1] *Lord Clarendon's Life*, p. 25.
[2] *Diary and Correspondence of John Evelyn*, London, 1850, vol. i. pp. 347 ff.

in the sacring of the King. Sheldon, now Bishop of London, was at the Archbishop's side in readiness to give him assistance if required, and to take the place of the venerable Primate on an emergency. The sermon was preached by Morley, Bishop of Worcester. Juxon was the first to salute the King on each cheek and to do homage. This was Archbishop Juxon's last appearance in public.

Whilst Juxon retained his office until his death on June 4, 1663, Sheldon, as Bishop of London, became in influence and authority Primate, advising and assisting Juxon, who consulted him freely, and he practically governed the Church in the Archbishop's name. During these three years in which Juxon was Primate, Gilbert Sheldon was a prelate of extraordinary importance ; and it is not a little remarkable that, outstanding as he was at a great crisis in the history and fortunes of the English Church, no attempt has hitherto been made to write his biography. Whilst the lives of very many Churchmen of the seventeenth century have been written, and their words and actions recorded in print—lives of men vastly inferior in point of influence to Gilbert Sheldon —no biographer has hitherto claimed the privilege of giving the Church any permanent record of the life of the most prominent bishop of the times of the Restoration.

A.D. 1661 is memorable as being the year in which was held the Savoy Conference, at which Gilbert Sheldon was destined to take a prominent part. When Charles II was at Breda, he had undertaken to make certain concessions to the presbyterian party in England, who were alike strong in numbers and in religious convictions.

"Careless and flexible as he was, he can hardly be said to have violated his word, when he appointed a conference to be held between them and the clergy, and when he deferred finally to the decision of Parliament. The nonconformists had presumed before this on the good nature of the King, and they pressed him so hard, that he could not refrain from giving utterance to his indignation. They had come to Breda to seek a toleration for themselves, which would have been tantamount to an amalgamation of the Church with dissent; and yet they urged the King to lay aside the Liturgy, or to abstain from using it in the royal chapel. The Liturgy had never been laid aside by lawful authority, and would nationally become, on the Restoration of the regal government, the order of public worship. The King, with some warmth, therefore replied, that while he gave them liberty, he could not have his own taken from him."[1]

[1] Hook, *Lives*, xi. 423. See Clarendon, *Hist. of Rebellion*, iii. 989.

The presbyterians then pressed the King with more importunity, that the use of the surplice might be discontinued by his Majesty's chaplains, inasmuch as the very sight of it would be an occasion of offence and scandal to the people. This request only served to increase the King's impatience at their intolerance. They found his Majesty as inexorable on this point as on the former; and he told them plainly—

"that he would not be restrained himself, when he gave others so much liberty; that the surplice had been always held a decent habit in the Church, constantly practised in England till these late ill times; that it had been still retained by him; and though he was bound for the present to tolerate much disorder and indecency in the exercise of God's worship, he would never in the least degree, by his own practice, discountenance the good old order of the Church in which he had been bred." [1]

From an English Churchman's point of view, the King's answers were quite admirable. Though much dissatisfied and disappointed at his Majesty's inflexibility, the presbyterians forebore troubling him further, hoping that when again in England they might find their opportunity. In this they were doomed to disappointment.

[1] See Cardwell, *Hist. of Conferences*, vi. 247.

Upon the return of Charles II to England, the use of the Book of Common Prayer of A.D. 1604 was at once restored in his chapel; and on March 25, 1661, a conference between clergy and presbyterians was appointed to be held under a royal Commission in the ancient and splendid hall of the Savoy Hospital, of which Sheldon, the Bishop of London, was Master. Twelve bishops and twelve nonconformist ministers were selected: nine of the number of each party were unable or unwilling to attend, and others were accordingly appointed to fill the vacancies.

The Savoy Conference was held under Archbishop Juxon's primacy, but he was unable to take part in it: as an old man, he naturally shrank from the hot discussions which were inevitable. The chief business, therefore, fell to the lot of Bishop Sheldon, now virtually primate. With admirable tact he carried the affair through; and, so far as the Church was concerned, with good taste and fine feeling, kept himself in the background, in his determination not to supplant the Archbishop, rarely putting in an appearance at the deliberations of the commissioners. The conference was limited in duration to four calendar months.[1] The record of the proceedings is given

---

[1] See Cardwell, *Hist. of Conferences*, vii. 300.

very fully and accurately by Dr. Edward Cardwell, in his invaluable work, the second edition of which was published by the University Press of Oxford, A.D. 1841, entitled : *A History of Conferences connected with the Revision of The Book of Common Prayer ; from the year* 1558 *to the year* 1690.[1]

The bishops, having obtained a copy of the proposals of the nonconformists, drew up their answer in detail. Burnet has observed that—

" Sheldon saw well what the effect would be of putting them (the nonconformists) to make all their demands at once. The number of them raised a mighty outcry against them, as people that could never be satisfied."[2]

It is very probable that such a result was foreseen and reckoned upon. In order to do justice to the controversy, the exceptions of the presbyterian party and the replies of the bishops must be read in detail.[3]

At the commencement, and during the early stage of the discussion, the bishops conducted themselves with patience and dignity. They

---

[1] Chapter vi., " The Proceedings of the Conference at the Savoy."
[2] Burnet, *Hist. of His Own Time*, i. 252.
[3] These will be found in full in Cardwell, *Hist. oj Conferences*, VII., v. vi. pp. 303–363. In the face of present discussions on a revision of the Book of Common Prayer, the account should be studied.

were there to take their proper position as judges and not as disputants. The case was simply one of plaintiff and defendant, to the obvious disadvantage of the former. The bishops expressed themselves ready to consider reasonable amendments of the existing Prayer Book of A.D. 1604, but not to make any drastic alterations. By the terms of the commission the current Book was to be regarded as the basis of any possible revision. The clergy, the Prayer Book and its ceremonies were in legal and rightful possession, which could not reasonably be disturbed or fettered. The royal warrant for the conference specified that the commissioners were

"to review the Book of Common Prayer, and to make such alterations therein as shall be thought most necessary, and some additional forms in the Scripture phrase, as near as might be, suited to the nature of the several parts of worship."[1]

The commissioners were instructed

"to advise upon and review the said Book of Common Prayer, comparing the same with the most ancient Liturgies which have been used in the Church in the primitive and purest times."[2]

[1] Cardwell, *Hist. of Conferences*, ch. vii., p. 299.
[2] *Ibid.*, p. 300.

The document was signed "Per ipsum Regem, Barker."

The Conference held at the Savoy achieved nothing : it ended on July 24, 1661, by the expiration of the four months' limit imposed upon the commissioners by the King's warrant. The strong current of public opinion had ever been in the direction of high prerogative and Church authority. Toleration, in any wide or extensive sense, was not possible; for the presbyterian party was as unwilling to accept it now at the hands of the Church party, as they had resolutely withheld it from their opponents when they themselves were in the ascendancy. Its supporters only created a storm of bitterness and scorn, by recalling the memories of that period of confusion and tyranny when their principles had unhappily prevailed.

We must now turn our attention to the legislative measures directed against the Puritans. At the Restoration the whole face of the nation was instantly changed. There was, be it in justice said, much in the Puritanism of the Commonwealth that was noble and good, even in its austerity; but all this was suddenly swept away as by a whirlwind, together with all that deserved to perish—the tyranny, narrowness, and even pettiness of Puritanism : the current of the people's hatred swiftly carried the whole Puritan structure away. Religion had been perverted to become a system of political and social despotism and tyranny, and it fell in ruins before the new order of things. And, moreover, England's animosity to Puritan ideals proceeded much further, even to the unworthy and short-sighted methods of so-called "religious" intolerance and persecution, which ever over-reach themselves and fail in their purpose.

The aid of the law was called in, and a series of bills was passed by the new "Cavalier Parliament" which breathe the fierce spirit of animosity and petty rancour against the men who had governed the nation during the Commonwealth. The eternal law of charity, even towards enemies, was profoundly violated in the name of religion, and a determination was openly manifested by the authorities in Church and State to avenge the twelve years of oppression which lasted from 1648 to 1660. The Cavaliers made up their minds to do as they had been done by. Summary measures were passed by Parliament, and enforced with the utmost severity. The Savoy Conference between representatives of the Church and the presbyterian parties was fruitless, and left things as they were before, neither side being prepared to make any concessions whatever. Parliament at once passed the Act of Uniformity (A.D. 1662), which left the presbyterians but one of two alternatives—either to conform, or to leave the Church. The presbyterian ministers, who had been intruded on the benefices and parishes of the English Church, were required to seek episcopal ordination and to assent to the Book of Common Prayer and the Thirty-nine Articles, on pain of deprivation. They were given till St. Bartholomew's Day, August 24, 1662, to make their decision.[1] This left but three months to choose between conformity or expulsion. As to the shortness of the time allowed for making their decision, they could hardly complain, for it exceeded that permitted by themselves to the clergy whom they expelled in the days of their power. For example, Gilbert Sheldon himself, as Walker relates,[2] had less than three days' notice to quit from the Oxford Visitors, and was then dispossessed. The ejected in 1662 had been themselves the ejectors but a few years previously, and it is quite impossible to recognise

[1] By 15 Car. 2, c. 6, the time was extended to Christmas Day, 1663.

[2] *Sufferings of the Clergy,* ii. p. 98.

any injustice in requiring the presbyterian in-
truders to make way for the original and rightful
owners, whom they had so mercilessly supplanted ;
they merely reaped as they had sown. A considerable number of the presbyterian ministers
conformed, and became the founders of the
" Low Church " school of thought in later times.
Others, to the number of about two thousand,
refused to conform, and were expelled from
their ill-gotten benefices and preferments on St.
Bartholomew's Day, A.D. 1662. Many of these
appear to have conformed later. Lord Clarendon,
who, though Chancellor, was an unwilling actor in
the affair, considered that the attitude of the
presbyterian ministers was largely one of " bluff,"
and adopted with the view to dramatic effect ;[1]
and he adds that "the greatest of them after
some time," when they found that private assistance began to diminish, "subscribed to those very
declarations which they had urged as the greatest
motives to their non-conformity." And he goes
on to say "the number was very small, and of
very weak and inconsiderable men, that continued

---

[1] Clarendon's opinion is supported by an extract from *Pepys'
Diary*, under September 3, 1662 : " Dr. Fairbrother told me that
most of the Presbyters now begin to wish they had complied, now
they see that no indulgence will be granted them, which they
hoped for."

refractory." Clarendon's testimony is of first-rate importance and veracity, for he was a chief agent in the business, and had the best means of knowing the real facts of the case. The presbyterians who refused to conform are the original founders of the Nonconformists or Dissenters of our own day. The Act of Uniformity was thoroughly and drastically enforced : the times were those in which there were no half-measures.

In our own day we hear much of these doings on "Black Bartholomew of 1662," and of the hardships inflicted upon the Nonconformists of the time. But there is another side of the picture which, in the interests of historical truth, should be well considered. If we regard the position of, and the treatment dealt out to, Churchmen during the years 1642 to 1660, when the presbyterians were in power, we shall recognise that a cruel and aggressive policy of oppression and persecution was carried out against them. And this certainly accounts very largely for the retribution which overtook the presbyterians at the Restoration. During the Commonwealth it is estimated that about eight thousand [1]

[1] "White boasted, he and his had ejected eight thousands"; but Walker, who wrote in 1714, computes the number as "in all probability a total nothing short of ten thousand."—*Sufferings*, Pt. I., pp. 199, 200.

clergymen of the English Church were expelled their benefices, either by force through not subscribing the Covenant, by orders of the Parliament, or at the hands of adventurers ready to fall upon the spoil. Numbers of the ejected clergy were cast into the gaols, and old ships were converted into prisons.[1]   A certain member of the Long Parliament, Rigby by name, actually made a contract for the sale of some of the clergy to be used as slaves on foreign plantations, and this ruffian twice introduced a motion that their transportation should be legalised.[2]   William Dugdale adds, that :

"Rigby not only exposed them to sale, but found purchasers also, and, what is more, had actually contracted with two merchants for them, and for that reason moved it twice (in the House, as I understood him) that they might be disposed of."[3]

[1] *Sufferings*, Pt. I., p. 57—"after they filled all the common jails and compters with them, they were forced to erect more new jails ... altho' they had likewise considerable numbers under confinement in the Ships.... Very many persons of very good quality, both of the clergy and laity, were committed to prison on board the Ships in the River of Thames, where they were kept under decks, and no friends suffered to come to them ; by which many lost their lives."
[2] *Life of Dr. John Barwick*, Lond., 1904, p. 42. *Querela Cantab.*, Oxon., 1646, p. 6.
[3] Quoted by Walker, *Sufferings, &c.*, Part I., p. 58. The original, however, is as follows—"Did not Mr. Rigby (a beloved Member) move twice that those Lords and Gentlemen which were Prisoners (for no cause but being Malignants, as they termed

This is confirmed by the two sons of Dr. Lay-field, Archdeacon of Essex, as Walker relates,[1] and he also mentions the intention of shipping the ejected clergy to Algiers, there to be sold for slaves to the Turks, as a monstrous and exquisite piece of cruelty.[2] Many of the suffering clergy fled the country and sought refuge on the continent or in Virginia. A promise of one-fifth of their own lawful means was 'generously' promised to the ejected clergy; but, in many cases, the promise was not fulfilled, and they had to earn their bread by acting as tutors and chaplains to the nobility. Paid agents were even employed for bringing false accusations against the clergy, in cases where it was found " that parishioners were not forward to complain of their ministers"; these agents were commonly ticketed "parson-hunters." In consequence of outbreaks of loyalty to the throne on the part of the Royalists, opportunities to act as tutors were closed to the deprived clergy by an Order of 1655, which brought them to destitution.

With these facts before us, we are enabled to

them) should be sold as Slaves to Argiere, or sent to the new Plantations in the West Indies, because he had contracted with two merchants for the purpose?"—Dugdale, *A Short View of the Late Troubles in England*, Oxford at the Theater, 1681, p. 577.

[1] *Sufferings, &c.*, Part I., p. 59.
[2] *Ibid.*, p. 58.

form a more just opinion as to the action of the authorities at the Restoration. As shedding some light upon the hardships and privations inflicted upon the clergy, it is significant that, at the Restoration, only about one-tenth of the number who had been forcibly deprived and ejected by the presbyterians came forward to claim their benefices—so great was the havoc caused by death and banishment at the hands of their persecutors. As to who the "martyrs" really were in these transactions, which were concluded by the Act of Uniformity, there cannot be a shadow of doubt—the "martyrs" were the clergy of the Church of England.

Having dealt with the Puritan ministers, Parliament proceeded to legislate against their lay adherents by means of the Corporation Act (A.D. 1661). This Act required all civil office-bearers to take the oath of supremacy and allegiance to the Crown, and to receive the Holy Communion according to the Prayer Book Rite. By this unfortunate Act the Eucharist, the Sacrament of Love, was prostituted and degraded to become a mere political test of loyalty to the throne.

Two further bills, drawn up by Parliament against the Puritans, remain to be briefly noticed.

F

(1) The Conventicle Act (A.D. 1664) prohibited assemblies of Nonconformists for religious purposes. Family prayers were permitted, provided that not more than four persons were present in addition to the household; beyond this number the meeting was deemed to be a 'conventicle,' and those who took part in it were liable to punishment. (2) The Five-Mile Act (A.D. 1665), which allowed no Puritan minister, who declined assent to the Act of Uniformity, to reside within five miles of any city or corporate borough.

As the Nonconformists were already fairly crushed and harmless to the Constitution, the legislation, which followed the Act of Uniformity, can only be described as vexatious and spiteful. Mr. Oman gives it as his opinion that :—

" The numbers of the Nonconformists were already rapidly dwindling, and by the end of the century they did not number a fifth of the population of the realm : the vast majority of them had gone to swell the Low Church party within the Anglican establishment." [1]

Attention to these Acts is called in these pages of the biography of Sheldon, because, whilst it is almost certain that he had the principal hand

[1] Oman, *Hist. of England*, 19th. ed. p. 424.

in their framing,[1] it is quite certain that he was active in rigidly enforcing them. We learn from Burnet[2] that there was a great discussion in Council, a little before St. Bartholomew's Day, 1662, whether the Act of Uniformity should be rigorously put into execution or not. Some desired delay, others were in favour of 'conniving at some eminent men' putting curates into their churches to read the Services of the Book of Common Prayer, yet leaving the greater offenders 'to preach on till they should die out.' Sheldon pressed for the execution of the law, on the ground that England was wont to obey laws, and urging that safety alone lay in obedience to authority. He also undertook to fill all vacancies that would occur in London with most able men, who would give great satisfaction as preachers.[3] He appears to have believed that, if a stout front was maintained, comparatively few of the

---

[1] "To Sheldon we owe the St. Bartholomew's Act, the Act of Uniformity, with those rigid clauses which we have now shaken off, and all those stern measures which made Puritanism a permanent and perpetual schism."—Milman, *St. Paul's*, Murray, Lond., 1879, p. 201.

[2] *Hist. of his Own Time*, vol. i. p. 268.

[3] "Dr. Fairbrother tells me, what I heard confirmed since, that it was fully resolved by the King's new Council that an Indulgence should be granted the Presbyters ; but upon the Bishop of London's (Gilbert Sheldon's) speech (who is now one of the most powerful men in England with the King) their minds were wholly turned."—*Diary and Correspondence of Samuel Pepys*, Lond., 1848, vol. ii. p. 30.

Puritan ministers would ultimately refuse to conform; and, according to Clarendon, he was not far wrong. Sheldon gained his point, and the Act of Uniformity was pressed upon the Puritan party with extreme rigour. In regard to the Five-Mile Act, Burnet says that:—

"Sheldon and Ward were the bishops that acted and argued most for this Act, which came to be called the Five-Mile Act." [1]

The bishops were not unanimously in favour of this Act, for Dr. Earl, Bishop of Salisbury, who was held in great esteem by the clergy and the King, strongly opposed it. [2]

In judging Sheldon's action in regard to the severe measures taken against the Puritan party, we must not forget the provocation he had suffered at their hands when, in 1648, he had been summarily and illegally ejected, deprived, and imprisoned. Great as he undoubtedly was, he had not attained to the summit of true greatness—the generous forgiveness of injuries and the magnanimous treatment of those who inflict them. We may perhaps plead in his favour his desire for the honour of the Church, which the

---

[1] *History of his Own Time*, vol. i. p. 315.
[2] *Ibid.*

Puritans had set at nought, and the memory of the murder of the King, whom he had served, at Whitehall on January 30, 1649, the year before he, too, suffered indignity and harsh treatment at their hands. To Sheldon and Clarendon fell the thankless yet responsible task of reorganising the government of Church and State. It is very doubtful if, in the whole course of English history, a more perilous and arduous piece of work had ever before to be faced and carried through. Obscured by fierce party spirit, few periods of English history are less understood. It was a period fairly bristling with complicated details; and, in the face of all this, we are at least in duty bound to remember that, whatever our own opinions may be as to the policy of Sheldon, and with him Clarendon his friend, it represented the will of the overwhelming majority of the English nation,[1] and that these two men understood, as few men of the time understood, the character

---

[1] "It was popular feeling that was so strong in suppressing nonconformity. All that was done, was done in accordance with the national will, and was at least as welcome to the laity as to the clergy. It is a well-known fact that the Act of Uniformity and the rest of the 'Clarendonian Code' would have been far less rigorous if they had been framed solely by the House of Lords where the Bishops in the flush of their regained power must have had great weight in such matters. It was in the House of Commons that the greatest intolerance prevailed."—Overton, *Life in the English Church*, Lond., 1885, p. 345.

of the abandoned and shifty sovereign with whom they had to reckon. Moreover, for many generations to come, the most liberal,statesmen found it advisable if not necessary to support the policy of Sheldon and Clarendon in regard to religious disabilities. And, lastly, in order to clear our judgment, it is an essential requisite to put our minds back some centuries, and so view the whole situation regardless of the difference of view produced by the lapse of time.

Of Sheldon's ability as a divine or his eminence as a preacher, we are unable to form any opinion ; but the scanty notices we have of him as the latter, seem to point to his possessing no special gifts. That this was the case is suggested by Sheldon not being chosen to preach the sermon at the coronation of King Charles II—that duty being assigned to Bishop Morley. We find that, on June 28, 1660, as Dean of the Chapel Royal, Dr. Sheldon preached before the King at Whitehall, on the day of solemn thanksgiving for his Majesty's restoration to the throne of England. Evelyn notes in his *Diary* that, on February 27, 1661, being Ash Wednesday—

"Preached before the King, the Bishop of London (Dr. Sheldon) on Matthew xviii. 25, concerning charity and forgiveness," his text being—

"But for as much as he had not to pay, his lord commanded him to be sold, and his wife, and children, and all that he had, and payment to be made."

The only printed works of Sheldon in the British Museum are:—(1) "Act of Parliament against religious meetings . . . or a letter of the Archbp. of Canterbury to his fellow Bishops" [London] 1670, 4to. (2) "David's Deliverance. . . . A Sermon," Lond., 1660, 4to (Press mark, 694 d, 19 [1], reprinted in Appendix IV. to this volume). The Bodleian Library, Oxford, has the latter, and also "A Letter to the Bishop of Lincoln," Oxf. 1670, fol. (Press mark, P. 1, 16 Jur.). Watts, in his *Bibliotheca Britannica* (Edin., 1824, vol. ii., 'Authors'), gives under 'Gilbert Sheldon,' "Sermon on the Restoration," Lond., 1660, 4to, and "Thanksgiving Sermon," Lond., 1660, 4to. Cardwell (*Documentary Annals*, vol. ii.) prints (1) "The Archbishop of Canterbury's letter to the bishop of London about nonconformists," A.D. 1665. (2) "The Archbishop of Canterbury's letter to the commissary, the dean, and archdeacon of Canterbury concerning the King's directions to the clergy," A.D. 1670.   (3) " The Archbishop of Canterbury's circular letter to cathedrals, that the residentiaries should in their own persons per-form divine service on Sundays and holidays at least," A.D. 1670.   The more important of these writings of Sheldon are reproduced later in this volume.

CHAPTER IV

THE REVISION OF THE PRAYER BOOK, A.D. 1661

Convocation summoned—Opening of Convocation at St. Paul's Cathedral—Sheldon appointed to preside—Preparations for revision of the Book of Common Prayer—Forms of Prayer for January 30 and May 29—Neglect of Baptism provided for through Sheldon's influence—Revision of the Book of Common Prayer — Details of alterations and additions adopted—Ratification of the revision by the Act of Uniformity—The revised Book subscribed by Convocation and accepted by the State.

SOON after the Restoration of Charles II a doubt was raised as to the expediency of summoning Convocation; but a powerful pamphlet, written by Dr. Heylin, Sub-Dean of Westminster, produced so profound an impression on the mind of Lord Clarendon, that Archbishop Juxon at once obtained his mandate for its assembling. In the house of Dr. Barwick, Dean of St. Paul's, was—

"an oratory, formerly consecrated to God, but profaned at the late rebellion, which he was at the charge of restoring to its antient beauty, and he constantly performed Divine service there, recommending to God the cause of the oppressed Church and King." [1]

In this oratory, in St. Paul's churchyard, on May 8, 1661, Dr. Sheldon, Bishop of London, with the Bishops of the Southern Province, and other clergy, assembled, and thence proceeded to Old St. Paul's Church. [2]

The renewal of the pageant surrounding the opening of Convocation, so long omitted, afforded delight to the nation. Judges in official robes, bishops in scarlet chimeres, accompanied by clergy, walked in long procession up the nave of Old St. Paul's, singing *Te Deum laudamus*. The prayers were said in Latin, and a sermon in the same language was preached by Dr. Pearce, and then the members adjourned to the Chapter-house. The Archbishop, Dr. Juxon, being too aged and infirm to be present, the Bishop of London, Dr. Sheldon, was appointed to act in his stead as president—

"The splendour of this opening of the Convocation of Canterbury stood in contrast with the opening of the Savoy Conference. There nothing was done but jangling and disputes ; whereas the great council of the Church, being in correspon-

[1] *Barwick's Life*, p. 170.
[2] *Kennett's Register*, p. 434.

dence with the Convocation of the northern province, deliberately proceeded to business, and had
for its object, not contention, but legislation."[1]

Whilst the Savoy Conference terminated on
July 24, 1661, it will be observed that the
assembling of Convocation on May 8 had already
taken place, and the bishops had in the interval
made preparations for such changes in the Book
of Common Prayer as they considered to be
expedient.

The first business taken in hand was to draw
up forms of prayer for May 29 and January 30,
the former being, by a strange coincidence, the
anniversary both of the birth of Charles II and
the restoration of the monarchy. This act was
in accordance with the spirit of the time, and
it was forced upon Convocation by the exuberant
loyalty displayed by the people in general, and
by both Houses of Parliament in particular. The
proceeding serves to emphasise the bond of
union then existing between Church and State,
after the unhappy and lamentable disunion of
the Commonwealth.

The increase of the fanatical sect of Anabaptists
had led to the gross neglect of religious ordinances, and of Holy Baptism in particular, and a

---

[1] Hook, *Lives of the Archbishops of Canterbury*, vol. xi. p. 430.

considerable number of persons had grown up unbaptized. Three of the bishops—Salisbury, Peterborough, and St. Asaph—were appointed to compile an office for the baptism of adults, as recommended by Dr. Sheldon. Some other slight alterations in the baptismal services were made. Some progress was made during the earlier sessions in examining portions of a code of canons.

In the session of November 21, the first session after the close of the Savoy Conference, the Convocation entered upon the more serious business for the which it was chiefly assembled, namely, the consideration and revision of the Prayer Book of A.D. 1604. Eight of the bishops, including Bishop Cosin of Durham and Bishop Wren of Ely, were requested to prepare the Prayer Book for revision. Cardwell states [1] that Convocation was—

"so earnest in this matter, and so clearly directed in their judgment, as well by the recent discussions as by the strong expression of public opinion that . . . they were able at once to supersede their newly-appointed committee, and to make considerable progress in the revision of the Liturgy at the same meeting."

[1] *History of Conferences,* viii. 371.

The clergy of the lower house were equally prompt and decided, and thus the work of revision went on apace—

"With labourers so earnest and so friendly, the whole work was speedily completed, though not before great impatience had been shown by the King and the houses of Parliament."[1]

The following are the chief changes and additions made in the revision of the Book of Common Prayer by the Convocation of 1661, over which Bishop Sheldon presided :—

A new Preface, composed by Sanderson, was adopted—"It hath been the wisdom of the Church of England . . . "; and the Kalendar was reconstructed, the commemorations of Ven. Bede and St. Alban being added, and the descriptions of black-letter holy days, taken from Cosin's "Collection of Private Devotions," set down. A Table of Vigils, Fasts and Days of Abstinence, drawn from the same source, was added to the Kalendar. The quotations from the Bible—the Psalter, the Ten Commandments, and certain parts of the Communion, excepted— were taken generally from the Authorised Version of 1611. The word "priest" was substituted for "minister" in the Absolution of the Choir

[1] Cardwell, *Hist. of Confer.*, viii. 371.

Offices. The five prayers, following the Collects, were printed at the close of Matins and Evensong. The allusions to "rebellion" and "schism" were made in the Litany. For "bishops, pastors, and ministers" were substituted "bishops, priests, and deacons." There were introduced two prayers for Embertide—the first being taken from Cosin's "Collection of Private Devotions," the second from the Scottish Prayer Book of 1637, and there placed at the end of the Litany. The Prayer for Parliament was added, dating from 1625, most probably composed by Laud, when Bishop of St. David's, and found in his "Summary of Devotions," amongst 'Prayers upon Sundry Publick Occasions,' with the marginal note referring to an Order of Fasting, *ob Pestem gravissimam*, A.D. 1625, the beginning and the ending being verbally identical with the form in the revised Book of 1661. There was also added the Prayer for All Sorts and Conditions of Men, to be said as a substitute for the Litany on non-Litany mornings. This prayer in its original form was probably longer than at present, as the word "Finally" suggests. It has been attributed to Dr. Peter Gunning, who was a prominent member of the Savoy Conference, and later Bishop of Chichester and of Ely : when

Master of St. John's College, Cambridge, he would not allow it to be said after noon, " because the Litany was never read then, the place of which it was supposed to supply." [1] There were added the General Thanksgiving, composed by Dr. Reynolds, Bishop of Norwich,[2] and a Thanksgiving for Peace. New Collects were added for the Third Sunday in Advent and for St. Stephen's Day.[3] Both these new Collects are abnormally addressed to our Lord Jesus Christ, thus unfortunately betraying a lack of liturgical knowledge, since all prayer and thanksgiving in the Eucharistic Service is normally addressed to the Eternal Father through the Son, whose memorial before the Father is made at the Eucharist. The Collect for Holy Innocents' Day was altered.[4] For the Sixth Sunday after the Epiphany a magnificent new Collect, Epistle

---

[1] See Dr. Bisse, *The Beauty of Holiness*, 7th ed., 1720, p. 97. I have set forth the evidence here fully in my edition of *Hierurgia Anglicana*, Delamore Press, 1904, vol. iii. pp. 182 ff.

[2] Cardwell, *Synodalia*, vol. ii. p. 658.

[3] Until 1661, the Collect for St. Stephen's day ran—" Grant us, O Lord, to learn to love our enemies, by the example of Thy martyr Saint Stephen, who prayed for his persecutors to Thee, which livest, &c."

[4] Until 1661, the Collect for the Innocents' Day was—"Almighty God, whose praise this day the young Innocents Thy witnesses have confessed and showed forth, not in speaking, but in dying; mortify and kill all vices in us, that in our conversation, our life may express Thy faith, which with our tongues we do confess: through Jesus Christ our Lord."

and Gospel were provided, also a Collect for Easter Even. In several places the word "congregation" gave way to the word "church." An Epistle was provided for the festival of the Presentation. A few of the Gospels were shortened, and the anthems announcing Easter were enlarged. In the service for Holy Communion, a commemoration of the faithful departed was added to the Prayer for the Church; and a direction was made for presenting the alms, and placing the elements upon the Holy Table. Before the Prayer of Consecration the rubric was inserted directing the celebrant so to order the elements that he may with decency break the bread and take the cup into his hands. The side rubrics of the Prayer of Consecration, commonly called "the Manual Acts" were added,[1]

---

[1] I have shown elsewhere ("Narrative of the Institution of the Eucharist and the Accompanying External Gestures"— *Irish Church Quarterly*, 1909) that the insertion of the Manual Acts is a most deplorable addition to the Prayer Book, for they emphasise a view of Consecration inconsistent with our Lord's institution. There is absolutely no ground whatever for assuming, as these directions assume, that He used the action of laying His hands upon the bread and wine, as He uttered the words, "This is My Body" . . . "This is My Blood." . . . These words were His formula of *Administration*, not of *Consecration*. Moreover, the direction to break the bread *before* consecrating it, is opposed to our Lord's institution: He brake it *after* Consecration. In truth, the directions contained in the rubrics concerning the Manual Acts are an unwarrantable interference with, and dislocation of, the proceeding adopted and inaugurated by our Lord at His institution of the Eucharist, and call loudly for drastic revision.

FRONTISPIECE OF PRAYER BOOK, A.D. 1662

also the form for consecrating additional bread and wine if required,[1] and the covering the Consecrated Elements after communicating the people with a fair linen cloth.

" The Order of the Council of 1552, respecting kneeling at Communion, which had been removed by Queen Elizabeth, was now replaced, but the words 'corporal presence' were substituted for 'real and essential presence,' and it thus became a defence of the doctrine of the Real Presence instead of a denial of it."[2]

In the final rubrics of the Communion was added the clause—"If any remain of that (the bread and wine) which was consecrated, it shall not be carried out of the church. . . ." This direction was certainly not made, as some have most unworthily argued, to prohibit reservation of the Eucharist for the Sick and Dying, but to prevent profanity. The like decree was in force before the sixteenth century, at a time when reservation for the Sick was universally practised.[3] The Ordinal received attention, for the

---

[1] Can any words of condemnation be too strong for this extraordinary direction to consecrate with a bare recital of our Lord's words of administration ; or for this permission to consecrate one element alone, apart from the other—a practice utterly wanting in liturgical or Catholic precedent?

[2] Procter and Frere, *New Hist. B. of C. Prayer*, p. 197.

[3] For the evidence, see *Hierurgia Anglicana*, ed. Staley, London, 1903, vol. ii. pp. 164, 165.

G

words " for the office and work of a priest," and
" for the office and work of a bishop," were added,
to be used at the laying on of hands in either
case.   This addition was made, not to supply any
supposed defect existing previously, but to meet
objections of the presbyterian party, who held that
the office of bishop and priest was identical.
The Preface to the Confirmation Service was
curtailed and amended ; the reception of the Holy
Communion on the day of marriage was no longer
insisted on as essential ; the clause " if he humbly
and heartily desire it " was added to the rubric
concerning absolution in the office for the Visitation of the Sick, with other additions to that
service ; the first rubric, referring to the unhap-
tized or excommunicate, was added to the Burial
office ; forms of prayer to be used at sea were
supplied ; and services for commemorating the
martyrdom of King Charles I (January 30), and
the restoration of King Charles II (May 29)
provided, and the former service for ' Papists'
Conspiracy ' (November 5) amended.

These and numerous minor or verbal alterations,[1] computed by Dr. Tennison to amount to
600 in number, were made in the Book of

[1] There is no more ready method of realising the changes made
in the Prayer Book in 1661, than to refer to a copy of the fac-
simile of the Black-letter Prayer Book of 1636, which contains the

Common Prayer by the Convocation of A.D. 1661, and were finally ratified by the Act of Uniformity,[1] of the following year.

On December 20, 1661, the revised Book of Common Prayer was received, approved, and subscribed, by the members of both houses of Convocation, so that the time occupied in its review was one month only. At the top of the signatures stands, " W : Cant :," followed by " Gilb. London " (Dr. Sheldon), and the names of the other eighteen bishops of the Province of Canterbury.[2]

The work of Convocation thus completed with admirable despatch was laid before King Charles II, who relegated it to the consideration of his Privy Council; thence it passed, with his Majesty's recommendation, to the Houses of Parliament, where the work of the Church be-

alterations, made by hand, at the last revision. It was from this Black-letter copy, with its marginal manuscript notes and alterations, that the authoritative copy of the Book of Common Prayer of 1661 was written out, and attached to the Act of Uniformity, 13 and 14 Car. II.; henceforward known as The Book Annexed.

[1] The revised Book of Common Prayer came into use on Sunday, August 17, 1662. Under this date John Evelyn (in his *Diary* has : "Aug. 17, 1662 ; Being the Sunday when the Common) Prayer-Book, reformed and ordered to be used for the future, was appointed to be read, and the solemn League and Covenant to be abjured by all the incumbents of England under penalty of losing their livings ; our vicar read it this morning."

[2] The signatures are reproduced in Plate facing page 100.

came part of the statute law of England. The Act of Uniformity received the royal assent on May 19, 1662; and the Lord High Chancellor, the Earl of Clarendon, was instructed to convey the thanks of the House of Lords to the bishops and other clergy assembled in Convocation, for their care and industry shown in their review and revision of the Book of Common Prayer—a work in which Gilbert Sheldon took a prominent part.

SIGNATURES, "BOOK ANNEXED," A.D. 1661

CHAPTER V

SHELDON, ARCHBISHOP OF CANTERBURY

Death of Archbishop Juxon—His burial—Gilbert Sheldon, Arch-
bishop of Canterbury—His translation to the primacy
described—Taxation of the clergy—Sheldon, Chancellor of
Oxford University—William Dugdale—Mock sermon before
Sheldon at Lambeth—Sheldon and All Souls, Oxford—
Anthony à Wood and Sheldon—Sheldon's patronage of men
of letters—Sheldon and Hooker—Marriage of the Duke of
Grafton—Letters of Archbishop Sheldon.

ON June 4, 1663, good Archbishop Juxon passed
to his rest. He had desired to be buried in the
place of his education, the chapel of St. John's
College, Oxford, to which he had bequeathed the
large sum of £500 a year ; and he had expressed
a wish to be buried without pomp or display.
His desire was disregarded, for a more ostenta-
tious and elaborate funeral has scarcely ever been
described. The hearse was drawn by six horses
with escutcheons on their foreheads and backs,
and attended by sixty horsemen ; the mourners
occupied fifteen coaches, thirteen of which were
drawn by six horses. Garter King-at-arms, with
four heralds in their tarbards, met the body on

its arrival at the Chapel. A ducal mitre, gilt, was
set at the head of the coffin, and at its foot a gilt
crozier. The ceremonial details of this extraordinarily pompous funeral may be read in Le
Neve, as communicated to him by Dr. Rawlinson.
Dr. Juxon had left £2000 to the repairs of St.
Paul's cathedral; his barge,[1] with its furniture,
he bequeathed to "his reverend brother, Gilbert,
Lord Bishop of London." Archbishop Juxon
had lived to see the completion of the revision
of the Prayer Book, and the passing of the Act
of Uniformity, which he was considerate in
enforcing. He had witnessed the overthrow of
the Church in the martyrdom of Archbishop
Laud and of King Charles the First, and its
restoration signified by the coronation of his son.
He had lived just long enough to see the vindi-
cation and triumph of the principles of which,
throughout a long and honourable life, he had
been the consistent advocate through evil report
and good report. And now for him—

> "Sunset and evening star:
> And one clear call for me."

It is said that, with characteristic humility,
Juxon steadfastly refused to sit for his portrait

---

[1] Dr. Wake, who died A.D. 1737, was the last archbishop who
went to Parliament by water.

to any artist, and that the pictures of him at
Long Leat and St. John's College, Oxford, were
executed from memory, the face being painted in
after death upon an adaptation of the Laudian
dress—a device commonly adopted at the time.
Juxon's lying-in-state for two days in the Divinity
School, Oxford, would afford facilities for this
being done. The expression is very sad, as if
echoes of that mysterious word "Remember,"
addressed at the last moment by the royal
martyr on the scaffold at Whitehall, were still
floating around him.

The mortal remains of William Juxon lie in
the chapel of St. John's College, Oxford, beside
those of his martyred predecessor in the See of
Canterbury. In the *History of the University of
Oxford*, published but a few years after Juxon's
death at the Sheldonian Press,[1] in the description
of St. John Baptist's College, we read :—

"Ad orientum hujus Capellæ, sub ipso Altari,
sunt quatuor cryptæ sive loculi non admodum
amplæ, in quibus horum, quos subjecimus,
reliquiæ conduntur. In primâ, ad parientem
borealem continentur ossa D. *Thomæ Whyte*,
Fundatoris. . . .

---

[1] *Historia et Antiquitates Universitatis Oxoniensis*, Oxoniæ e
Theatro Sheldoniano, MDCLXXIV., lib. ii. fol. 314.

" In proxima et huic pene contigua, requiescunt cineres R. P. *Gulielm. Laud* Archiepiscopi *Cantuariensis*, translati ex Ecclesiâ *Omnium Sanctorum* de BARKING juxta Turrim *Lond.* et hic depositi, xxiv Julii MDCLXIII. . . .

" In tertia, reconditur R. P. *Gulielmus Juxon* Archiepiscopus Cantuariensis, sepultus ix. Julii MDCLXIII. in hujus capuli exteriori parte, laminæ affixæ hæc inciduntur. *Depositum Reverendiss. in Christo Patris Gulielmi Archiepiscopi Cantuariensis, qui moriebatur iv. Jun.* MDCLXIII.

" In quarta reconduntur ossa Doctoris *Richardii Baylie*, nuper Præsidentis."

At the foot of Loggan's plate of St. John the Baptist's College, published in 1674, Juxon is described as

" Illustrissimus Dominus D. Guilielmus Iuxon, D. Laudum, tantū exemplar, per omnes Virtutū et Dignitatū gradus ad Primatū usque secutus. . . ."

And so we leave the ashes of these two great Archbishops lying side by side in the chapel of St. John the Baptist's College. And what a meeting of these two eminent servants of God beyond the veil! Was it left to Juxon to bring the tidings of the restoration of the Church to him who had, with their martyred royal master, laid his head on the block to save it? Who can tell?

By the death of Archbishop Juxon the See

of Canterbury became vacant, and it must have been the general expectation that Gilbert Sheldon would be called to fill it. ,He was undoubtedly the most prominent and capable ecclesiastic of the time, high in the favour of King Charles II, and Lord Clarendon, his chief minister; and, moreover, during the closing year of Juxon's life, Sheldon had practically governed the Church. He had taken the leading part in the controversy with the Puritan party at the Savoy Conference, and had been called to take the Archbishop's place as president of the Convocation in which the Book of Common Prayer was revised and re-imposed by the Act of Uniformity of 1662. It must have been a foregone conclusion, therefore, that Gilbert Sheldon, who had succeeded William Juxon in the See of London, would be destined to succeed him in the chair of Augustine. And so it fell out.

On August 11, 1663, Sheldon was elected to the primacy, and three weeks later, August 31, the translation was completed in the Archbishop's Chapel, Lambeth. He was then sixty-five years of age, and he held the primacy until his eightieth year.[1]

[1] W. E. Gladstone remarks, "I cannot find that from the time of Archbishop Sheldon anyone has assumed the primacy at so great an age as seventy. Juxon, the predecessor of Sheldon, was

John Evelyn, in his *Diary*, August 31, 1663, states that he was present at Dr. Sheldon's translation from the See of London to that of Canterbury—

"I was invited to the translation of Dr. Sheldon, Bishop of London, from that See to Canterbury; the ceremony was performed at Lambeth. First, went his Grace's mace-bearer, steward, treasurer, comptroller, all in their gowns, and with white staves; next, the Bishops in their habits, eight in number; Dr. Sweate, Dean of the Arches, Dr. Exton, Judge of the Admiralty, Sir William Merick, Judge of the Prerogative Court, with divers advocates in scarlet. After divine service in the chapel, performed with music extraordinary, Dr. French and Dr. Stradbury (his Grace's chaplains) said prayers. The Archbishop in a private room looking into the chapel, the Bishops who were commissioners went up to a table placed before the altar, and sat round it in chairs. Then, Dr. Chaworth presented the commission under the broad seal to the Bishop of Winchester, and it was read by Dr. Sweate. After which, the Vicar-General went to the vestry, and brought his Grace into the chapel, his other officers marching before. He being presented to the Commissioners, was seated in a

much older; but his case was altogether peculiar."—Morley, *Life of W. E. Gladstone*, vol. iii. pp. 95, 96. Mr. Gladstone appears to have made a slip here in regard to Sheldon's age.

great arm-chair at one end of the table, when the definitive sentence was read by the Bishop of Winchester, and subscribed by all the Bishops, and proclamation was three times made at the chapel door, which was then set open for any to enter, and give their exceptions; if any they had. This done, we all went to dinner in the great hall to a mighty feast. There were present all the nobility in town, the Lord Mayor of London, Sheriffs, Duke of Albemarle, &c. My Lord Archbishop did in particular most civilly welcome me."[1]

In the year 1664, by an arrangement made between Sheldon and Clarendon, a most important change was effected in regard to the clergy and Convocation, which, later, Dr. Edmund Gibson, Bishop of London (A.D. 1720–48) described as being "the greatest alteration in the constitution ever made without an express law." Hitherto, the clergy had taxed themselves in their synod, their proceedings being later confirmed by Parliament. By the arrangement arrived at between the Archbishop and the Lord Chancellor, the clergy silently waived the privilege of taxing themselves, submitting to be included in the money-bills of the House of Commons. The

---

[1] *Diary and Correspondence of John Evelyn*, Lond., 1850, vol. i. pp. 376, 377.

bill passed on this occasion was named, "An Act for granting a royal aid unto the King's Majesty," and it was the first in which the clergy were included. It is not easy to determine whether this great change was more to the interest or to the prejudice of the clergy of the Church of England.[1]

On the banishment of Lord Clarendon[2] in 1667, Gilbert Sheldon was elected Chancellor of the University of Oxford, with but one adverse vote. Among the Sheldon Papers in the British Museum[3] is a letter from the Archbishop, in which he declines the office on the score of a "crazy head and infirm health." This refusal he recalled later, and, in spite of physical infirmity, served in the office for two years. From stress of increasing infirmities Sheldon resigned the Chancellorship in 1669, and, on his pressing recommendation, the Duke of Ormond was chosen to succeed him—such was Sheldon's influence at Oxford. Anthony à Wood states that Sheldon

---

[1] See Lathbury, *A Hist. of the Convocation of the Church of England*, 2nd ed., p. 308 ; also Johnson, *The Clergyman's Vade Mecum*, Lond., 1715, pp. 158-9.

[2] Evelyn relates, "August 27th, 1667: Visited the Lord Chancellor, to whom his Majesty had sent for the seals a few days before ; I found him in his bedchamber very sad. The Parliament had accused him, and he had enemies at Court, especially the buffoons and ladies of pleasure, because he thwarted some of them, and stood in their way."—*Evelyn's Diary*, vol. ii. p. 28.

[3] Harleian MSS., cod. 3783$\frac{79}{109}$.

was never installed, nor ever after visited Oxford, "no not so much as to see his noble Work call'd the Theatre,"[1] and he repeats the same statement in regard to Canterbury.[2]

In a letter dated February 15, 1669–70, written by William Dugdale to Anthony à Wood,[3] we find that search was made in Prynne's study "for the finding out of those papers which were by him taken from that most reverend and renowned Prelate Arch-B[pp] Laud (whose memory ought to be highly honoured by all good men)." These papers included Laud's Diary, "which he the said Prynne unwarrantably got into his custody" (Wood's *Athenæ Oxon.*, ed., Bliss. iii. 874), which diary with "all those papers which they could finde" were delivered by Dugdale "to the Arch-B[pp] of Canterbury (Sheldon), and presented to his Hands."

Of Gilbert Sheldon as Archbishop of Canterbury there is not much to relate beyond what is recorded in the next chapter. But the following incident, painful as it is, must not be withheld, in the interests of impartiality and historical veracity.

---

[1] *Athen. Oxon.*, vol. ii. p. 1163.
[2] *Ibid.*
[3] *Life, Diary, and Correspondence of Sir W. Dugdale*, Lond., 1827, p. 390.

Samuel Pepys, in his *Diary*, under May 14, 1669, wrote—

"At noon with M^r. Wren, to Lambeth, to dinner with the Archbishop of Canterbury; the first time I was ever there, and I have long longed for it; where a noble house, and well furnished with good pictures and furniture, and noble attendance in good order, and a great deal of company, though an ordinary day, and exceeding great cheer, no where better, or so much, that ever I saw, for an ordinary table : and the Bishop (*sic*) mighty kind to me particularly, desiring my company another time, when less company there. Most of the company gone, and I was going, I heard by a gentleman of a sermon that was to be preached there ; and so I staid to hear it, thinking it serious, till by and by the gentlemen told me it was a mockery, by one Cornet Bolton, a very gentleman-like man, that behind a chair did pray and preach like a Presbyter Scot, with all possible imitation in grimaces and voice. And his text about the hanging up their harps upon willows (Psalm cxxxvii. 2) ; and a serious good sermon too, exclaiming against Bishops, and crying up my good Lord Eglinton, till it made us all burst; but I did wonder to have the Bishop at this time to make sport with things of this kind, but I perceive it was shown him as a rarity; and he took care to have the room-door shut, but there were about twenty gentlemen there, and myself, infinitely pleased with the novelty." [1]

The person referred to as "my good Lord Eglinton" appears to have been Alexander Montgomery, called Greysteel, a fierce presbyterian, and a ruling elder of the General Assembly, when the solemn League and Covenant were drawn up : he fought against Charles at Marston Moor, but eventually became a Royalist, dying at the age of seventy-three years in 1661. His son was a consistent supporter of the Monarchy, and there seems to be no reason why Eglinton should have been made an object of satire at this unseemly scene at Lambeth. That Sheldon should have stooped to listen to this mock sermon of a Cavalier, who held up the Puritan phrase and twang to ridicule, is a subject for deep regret. Some allowance must be made for the times when, as a rebound from the severity of Puritan ideals, sobriety in dress, speech, and manners were flouted as a mark of the detested Puritanism.

From the *Life* of the eccentric antiquarian, Anthony à Wood, Archbishop Sheldon's contemporary, we obtain some information regarding his connection with All Souls College, Oxford,

[1] *Diary and Correspondence of Samuel Pepys*, Lond., 1879, vol. vi. pp. 81, 82.

of which Sheldon was Visitor. The college had run considerably into debt. Sheldon was appealed to. "The Warden Sr Thomas is therefore chid and reprehended by the Archbishop." [1] This took place in 1671.

Under "A.D. 1669, 20 Car. II., Aug. 25," Wood writes:

" A. W. went about 8 of the clock in the Morning by Whitehall towards Sr John Cotton's House neare Westminster-hall, to borrow some MSS. from his Library, to carry on the ground work of the Hist. and Antiq. of the Univ. of Oxon. He met neare Whitehall Gate with Dr. Joh. Fell, Dr. Rich. Allestrie, Dr. Tho. Yate, etc. comming from Prayers, as it seems, at Whitehall, who told him, that at 12 of the clock of the said Day, he was to meet the Oxford Scholars then in London, to dine with his Grace the Archb. of Canterbury (Sheldon) at Lambeth. They told him then, that if he met by chance with any Oxford Doctors or Masters, between that time and 12 of the Clock, he should tell them of it, which he did. Afterwards he borrowed certaine MSS. and at 12 of the Clock he passed over the Water to Lambeth with Dr. Yate, Proctor Alsop and others. When they came there, the Archb. was at the Councill Table at Whitehall with the King, and did not returne till one of the Clock.

---

[1] *The Life of Anthony à Wood, from the year* 1632 *to* 1672, Oxford, 1772, p. 172.

CHARLES II WITH SHELDON AND CLARENDON

In the meane time the Doctors and Masters entertained themselves with Pictures and other Rarities in the Gallery and had divers Discourses. At length the Archb. came among them with Dr. Fell, and at their first entrie into the Gallery, A. W. being next to the Dore, Dr. Fell said to the Archbishop: *If it please your Grace, here is a Master of Arts* (pointing to A. W.) *that you must take notice of. He hath done the Universitie a great deal of honour by a Book that he hath written.* Whereupon the Archb. comming towards him, A. W. kneeled downe, and he bless'd him, and laying his hand upon his Shoulder when he was risen, spoke very kindly to him, and told him, that *he was glad that there was such a person in the Universitie, that had a generous mind to such a work.* He bid him to proceed in his Studies, that *he should be encourag'd, and want nothing that was equal to his Deserts.*" [1]

Again, under "A.D. 1671, 22 Car. II., Feb. 9–16," Anthony à Wood has—

"Sunday, Sr Leol. Jenkyns took with him in the Morn. over Water to Lambeth A. Wood, and after Prayers he conducted him up to the dining Rome, where Archb. Sheldon receiv'd him, and gave him his blessing. There then dined among the Company, Joh. Echard, the Author of *The Contempt of the Clergy*, who sate at the Lower

---

[1] *The Life of Anthony à Wood, from the year 1632 to 1672,* Oxford, 1772, pp. 221, 222.

H

end of the Table between the Archbishop's two Chaplays Sam. Parker and Tho. Thomkins, being the first time the said Echard was introduced into the said Archbishop's company. After Dinner the Archbishop went into his withdrawing Roome, and Echard with the Chaplaynes and Ralph Stow to their Lodgings to drink and smoak. Sr L. Jenkyns took then A. W. by the hand, and conducted him into the withdrawing Roome to the Archbishop; at which time desiring him to produce the 12 printed sheets of his book, (which he had carried with him from Oxon. by the advice of Dr. Fell) he thereupon put them into the hands of Sr Leolin, and Sr Leolin into the hands of the Archbishop, who spending some time upon them, liked well the character and paper, and gave A. W. great encouragement to proceed in his studies. After the returne of A. W. to Exeter house, Sr Leolin, who came after, told him, that he would warrant him an ample Reward, if he would present a fair copie bound to the Archb. when the Book was finish'd, etc. . . ."[1]

The book referred to in the foregoing extract was entitled *Historia et Antiquitates Universitatis Oxoniensis*, magnificently printed in folio at the Press of the Sheldonian Theatre in 1674, to which reference has already been made in the

[1] *The Life of Anthony à Wood, from the year* 1632 *to* 1672, Oxford, 1772, pp. 247, 248.

present work. The companion volume, *Oxonia Illustrata*, containing David Loggan's series of splendid engravings, was published at the same Press in 1675, and from this latter volume several illustrations in this *Life of Sheldon* are taken.

That Gilbert Sheldon was a patron of men of letters, and a man to whose encouragement and practical help literature owes a great debt, we also learn from the *Life of Sir William Dugdale*,[1] the antiquarian, who was—

"much importuned by the late Arch B'pp of Canterbury, Dr. Sheldon, and the then Earle of Clarendon, to perfect that Collection, begun by the learned Sr Henry Spelman, for his intended second volume of the Provinciall Councills here in England";

and that Sheldon contributed £40 towards the charges for printing the work. Moreover, it is not generally known that we owe the quaintly and exquisitely written *Life of Richard Hooker*, by Isaac Walton, to the influence and encouragement of Sheldon. Dr. Gauden, who died in 1662, was desired by Dr. Sheldon, when Bishop of London, to write and publish an account of "Master Hooker's" career and writings. This Life bore great marks of haste, and was not

[1] Lond. 1827, pp. 29, 359.

correct in some respects.[1]   Sheldon was so anxious that full justice should be done to Hooker, that he requested Walton to write a fresh and more accurate account of the great divine.   Walton began his *Life of Hooker* thus—

" I have been persuaded by a friend (Dr. Sheldon), whom I reverence, and ought to obey, to write *The Life of* Richard Hooker, the happy author of five (if not more) of the eight learned books of *The Laws of Ecclesiastical Polity*.[2]

In the Epistle to the Reader, prefixed to Walton's *Lives of Donne, Wotton, Hooker, and Herbert*, when first collected in 1670 into one volume, Walton says—

" Having writ these two lives (of Dr. Donne and Sir H. Wotton), I lay quiet twenty years, without a thought of either troubling myself or others, by any new engagement of this kind, for I thought I knew my unfitness.   But, about that time, Dr. Gauden (then Lord Bishop of Exeter), publisht *the Life of Mr. Richard Hooker* (so he called it), with so many dangerous mistakes, both of him and his books, that discoursing of them with his Grace, Gilbert [Sheldon] that now is Lord Arch-

---

[1] Isaac Walton, *Life of Mr. Richard Hooker*, in " Hooker's Works," 7th ed., Oxford, 1888, vol. i. p. 1, note.
[2] *Ibid.*, p. 3.

bishop of Canterbury, he enjoined me to examine some circumstances, and then rectify the bishop's mistakes, by giving the world a fuller and a truer account of Mr. Hooker and his books, than that bishop had done; and, I know I have done so. And, let me tell the reader, that till his Grace had laid this injunction upon me, I could not admit a thought of any fitness in me to undertake it; but, when he had twice enjoined me to it, I then declined my own, and trusted his judgment, and submitted to his commands; concluding, that if I did not, I could not forbear accusing myself of disobedience; and, indeed, of ingratitude for his many favours. Thus I became engaged into the third life."[1]

This incident discloses both the justice and the kindness of Archbishop Sheldon, and it is a pleasure to relate it.

In the year 1672 we find a brief reference to the Archbishop in Evelyn's *Diary*, under August 1, as follows—

" I was at the marriage of Lord Arlington's only daughter (a sweet child if ever there was any) to the Duke of Grafton, the King's natural son by the Duchess of Cleveland; the Archbishop of Canterbury officiating, the King and all the

---

[1] Isaac Walton, *Life of Mr. Richard Hooker*, in "Hooker's Works," 7th ed., Oxford, 1888, vol. i. p. 3, note. The above is quoted from the edition of 1675.

grandees being present. I had a favour given me by my Lady; but took no great joy at the thing for many reasons."[1]

The child was then only five years of age! What it must have cost Archbishop Sheldon to perform this marriage ceremony, it is not difficult to imagine: we should not have been surprised to know that he had, for obvious reasons, refused to officiate.

Few letters are more admirable than one of the last written by Archbishop Sheldon, which, after his death, was placed in the hands of his successor, Sancroft, in which Sheldon quite touchingly expostulates with an obstinately non-resident bishop on his gross dereliction of duty.[2] The exact date of this letter is unknown.

"My Lord,—Since neither ye duty you owe to your Dioces as you are a Bp̃ nor any thing y^t I have said to you by word of mouth has been preualent to carrie you down to your Bp̃rique to make yor personal Residence there; that thereby ye seueral ends for w'ch you were ordayn'd a Bp̃ might be fullfill'd, but that you still remayn in and about London without any just cause y^t you have made appear to mee: I have thought fitt by writing to you at this time upon ye same subject to

---

[1] *Diary and Correspondence of John Evelyn*, Lond., 1850, p. 77.
[2] Tanner MSS. vol. 36, fol. 190. Bodleian Lib., Oxford.

shew you how serious I am in y^t particular, and to tell you once more y^t I do expect you should forthwith and without any delay go down to your Bp̃rique and make yor Residence there, for if you will not perform y^t Episcopal duty y^t is incumbent upon you, yet I must and ought to do y^t wch' lyes upon me as I 'am you^r Metropolitan, w'ch is to see y^t done by you, w'ch you do so grossly neglect, and wch yor Episcopal Function requires at yor hands. Since therefore I do hereby require no more from you than what by ye nature of yor function or ye Laws Ecclĩcal of this nation you are to perform I do expect that you should comply therewith and put ye same presently in execution. And Albeit I should be very unwilling to take any publique rigorous course with you yet if this wch' I now require from you be not obey'd forthwith you must expect to hear further from me in an other way w'ch if it puts you to any open shame it is yor own fault when gentler means were used thyet (?) could not preuayl."

All through a long life Sheldon had ridden the storm. His times were those of turmoil and conflict. His motto might well have been, "Woe is me, for I am a man of strife"—strife with corrupt practices at All Souls College for long years, strife with revolutionaries and parliamentary visitors in the reign of Charles I and during the Commonwealth, strife with the Royal Martyr's unworthy successor in the throne and his corrupt Court, strife with the Puritans. Sheldon's career is reminiscent of the times of Nehemiah, when the builders of the walls of Jerusalem held a trowel in one hand and a weapon in the other. His career was one of strenuous activity and conflict; and he was a man, whatever his limitations and failings might be, who did not live in vain or shirk the warfare of life.

There are three official letters of Archbishop Sheldon which have been preserved to us, which should not be omitted from any full account of his life, and which are reprinted in the following pages of this biography.

(i) The first is entitled, "The Archbishop of Canterbury's letter to the Bishop of London about Nonconformists."[1] The orders and instructions accompanying this letter had two objects in view, namely, the improvement of the conforming clergy and the suppression of nonconformity. The discipline of the Church had fallen to a very low level as the result of the disorders of the Commonwealth. Amongst the opponents of the Church system were men mostly of moral character and religious profession, whilst amongst its adherents were the members of a

[1] *Reg. Sheldon*, fol. 205.

most dissolute and irreligious Court. Undue
ordination, loose profanity, glaring simony, non-
residence, and increasing pluralities prevailed.[1]
The first letter of Archbishop Sheldon with its
orders and instructions is as follows—

" Right reverend, and my very good lord. After
my hearty commendations, etc. Having heard
frequent complaints from many parts of my province, not only of great disorders and disturbances caused by the crafty insinuations and
turbulent practices of factious nonconformist
ministers, and other disaffected to the government of the church, but also of divers unworthy
persons, that even of late years have crept into
the ministry, to the scandal of the church, and
dissatisfaction of good men, a great part of which
miscarriages are imputed to the easiness, or inad-
vertency at least, of the bishops, who ought to
have a watchful eye against such growing mischiefs ; I have therefore thought good, as in like
cases hath often been done by my predecessors,
to recommend to your lordship, and the rest of
my brethren, the bishops of my province, the
orders and instructions herewithal sent, desiring
and requiring your lordship and them duly to
observe the same, and to give unto me such
account and certificates, as are thereby required.
Which that it may be performed, I desire your

[1] All this is set forth in a pamphlet printed at Cambridge in
1663, " Ichabod or five groans of the Church."

lordship, that you will impart the tenor of this my letter, together with a true copy of the said orders and instructions, to every one of my brethren, the bishops of my province, with all convenient speed. And so I bid your lordship heartily farewell.—Your lordship's very affectionate friend and brother, GILB. CANT.

".LAMBETH, *July* 7,
 MDCLXV.

"*Postscript.*—I desire that your lordship, in your letters to my brethren the bishops, will quicken them to make a speedy return to his majesty's instructions, for inquiries concerning hospitals, by me lately sent, and recommended to your lordship and them by his majesty's command."

I. *Concerning ordinations.*

" That all and every the said bishops within their several dioceses and jurisdictions be very careful what persons they receive into the ministry ; and that none be admitted into holy orders, unless he bring with him letters dimissory, according to the 34th canon ; and that no bishop, being not within his own proper diocese, do at any time hereafter confer orders upon any person without license first from us obtained ; and that in all things the canons concerning ordination be duly and punctually observed ; and that once every year, videlicet, within thirty days after the feast of the annunciation of our blessed lady St. Mary the virgin, every bishop do certify unto us the names, degrees, titles, and orders of every person by him ordained, within the year before, ending at Christmas then last past.

II. *Concerning pluralists and their curates.*

" That before the feast day of the annunciation of our blessed lady St. Mary the virgin next coming, they and every of them certify to me particularly the names, surnames, and degrees of all clergymen, that, together with any benefice with cure, do hold also any prebend, or ecclesias tical dignity, or promotion, or sinecure with the names and places of the said benefices, prebends, dignities, promotions, and sinecures ; and also the names, surnames, and degrees of all clergy- men, that hold two or more ecclesiastical bene- fices, with or without cure, whether within the same diocese, or in several dioceses, and the names and places wherein the said benefices are, and within what distance, or commonly reputed distance of miles ; and whether they hold the same by lawful qualification and dispensation ; and upon which of their benefices, prebends, dignities, or promotions they do reside ; and whether they keep and maintain able, orthodox, and conformable curates upon the said benefices, where they do not reside ; and whether any of them keep any curate, where they themselves do usually reside; and what are the names, surnames, and degrees of the said curates, and whether they be licensed and approved by the bishop, as they ought.

III. *Concerning lectures and lecturers.*

"That before the said feast day of our blessed lady St. Mary the virgin, they and every of them particularly certify unto me, what lectures are set up, and lecturers maintained within their respective dioceses; in what towns, places, and churches the same are set up; what allowances are made and established for any such lectures; what are the names, surnames, degrees, and qualities of all and every such lecturers; and whether such lectures be set up by and with the consent of the bishop of the diocese; and whether the said lecturers be lawfully licensed preachers, and by whom; and how they appear affected to the government of his majesty, and the doctrine and discipline of the church of England.

IV. *Concerning schoolmasters and instructors of youth.*

"That before the said feast day of our blessed lady St. Mary the virgin, they and every of them particularly certify me, how many, and what free schools are within their respective dioceses, and where, and by whom founded, and how endowed, and the names, surnames, and degrees of the schoolmasters and ushers in the said free schools; and also the names, surnames, and degrees of all other public schoolmasters, and ushers, or instructors, and teachers of youth in reading, writing, grammar, or other literature, and whether they be licensed, and by whom; as also of all public mistresses of schools and instructors and teachers of young maids or women; and of all other men and women, that keep scholars in their houses to board or sojourn, and privately teach them or others within their houses; and whether the said schoolmasters, ushers, schoolmistresses, and instructors, or teachers of youth publicly or privately, do themselves frequent the public prayers of the church, and cause their scholars to do the same; and whether they appear well affected to the government of his majesty and the doctrine and discipline of the church of England.

V. *Concerning practisers of physic.*

" That before the said feast day of our blessed lady St. Mary the virgin, they and every of them particularly certify me the names, surnames, degrees, and qualities of all practisers of physic within their respective dioceses; in what towns, villages, or places they live; whether licensed, and by whom; and how they appear affected to his majesty's government, and the doctrine and discipline of the church of England.

VI. *Concerning nonconformist ministers.*

" That before the feast of —— they and every of them particularly certify me the names, surnames, and degrees of all nonconformist ministers, that within their respective dioceses have been ejected out of any ecclesiastical benefice, promotion, or charge for nonsubscription, or nonconformity ; and where, and how, and in what profession of life they now do live ; and how they behave themselves in relation to the peace and quiet as well of the church, as of the state ; and further, if any such like nonconformist shall have removed from any other diocese into any of their respective dioceses, that they certify the same things concerning them, as well as of the others, in this instruction mentioned.   Given at my manor house at Lambeth in the county of Surrey, July the 7th, MDCLXV."

(ii) The second letter bears the title, " The Archbishop of Canterbury's letter to the Commissary, the Dean, and Archdeacon of Canterbury concerning the King's direction to the Clergy." [1]   Under the guidance of such men as Baxter and Manton, and with the support, given

---

[1] *Ex autographo penes Thom. episc. Assaven.*

secretly, of Charles II and his courtiers, the Nonconformists persisted in holding their religious meetings, until the passing of the Act for suppressing seditious conventicles was renewed A.D. 1670.[1] To this Act Archbishop Sheldon alludes in the following letter—

Right worshipful Mr. commissary, and right reverend Mr. dean, and Mr. archdeacon.

" It having pleased his majesty and the two houses of parliament, out of their pious care for the welfare of this church and kingdom, by making and publishing the late act for preventing and suppressing conventicles, to lay a hopeful way for the peace and settlement of the church, and the uniformity of God's service in the same ; it becomes us the bishops, ecclesiastical judges, and clergy, as most particularly sensible of the good providence of God, to endeavour, as much as in us lies, the promoting so blessed a work. And therefore having well considered what will be proper for me in my place to do, I have thought fit and do hereby recommend unto you, as my commissioners, jointly and severally these counsels and methods, which I desire, that in my stead, throughout my particular diocese of Cant. as well in places exempt as not exempt, you will pursue ; and which I have also by my letters given in

[1] 22 Charles II, c. 1.

charge to all the rest of my brethren, the bishops of my province, being thereunto encouraged by his majesty's approbation and express direction in this affair.

" In the first place therefore I advise and re-quire you, that you will call before you not only all officials, registers, and other ecclesiastical officers within my diocese; but that also by such means, and at such places as you shall judge most convenient, you assemble before you or some one or more of you the several parsons, vicars, and curates of my diocese and jurisdiction within their several deaneries; and that you im-part unto them respectively, as they shall come before you, the tenor of these my letters, re-quiring them in my name, that in their several capacities and stations they all perform their duty towards God, the king, and the church, by an exemplary conformity in their own persons and practice to his majesty's laws, and the rules of the church in this behalf.

"Secondly I advise, that you admonish and recommend to all and every of the parsons, vicars, and curates within my said diocese and jurisdic-tion strictness and sobriety of life and conversa-tion, checking and punishing such as transgress, and encouraging such as live orderly; that so by their virtue and religious deportment they may shew themselves patterns of good living to the people under their charge. And next, that you require of them, as they will answer the contrary, that in their own persons in their churches they do decently and solemnly perform the divine service by reading the prayers of the church, as they are appointed and ordered in and by the book of Common Prayer, without addition to or diminishing from the same, or varying, either in substance or ceremony, from the order and method, which by the said book is set down, wherein I hear and am afraid, too many do offend ; and that in the time of such their officiating, they ever make use of, and wear their priestly habit, the surplice and hood ; that so by their due and reverent performance of so holy a worship, they may give honour to God, and by their own example instruct the people of their parishes, what they ought to teach them in their doctrine.

" **Thirdly,** having thus counselled the ecclesiastical officers and clergy of my diocese in their own particular duties, you are further desired to recommend unto them the care of the people under their respective jurisdictions and charges, that in their several places they do their best to persuade and win all nonconformists and dissenters to obedience to his majesty's laws, and unity with the church ; and such as shall be refractory, to endeavour to reduce by the censures of the church, or such other good means and ways as shall be most conducing thereunto.

" To which end, I advise that all and every of the said ecclesiastical judges and officers, and all, and every of the clergy of my diocese, and the churchwardens of every parish by their respective ministers be desired in their respective stations and places, that they take notice of all nonconformists, holders, frequenters, maintainers, and abettors of conventicles and unlawful assemblies, under pretence of religious worship, especially of the preachers and teachers in them, and of the place wherein the same are held, ever keeping a most watchful eye over the cities and greater towns, from whence the mischief is for the most part derived into the lesser villages and hamlets. And wherever they find such wilful offenders, that then with a hearty affection to the worship of God, the honour of the king and his laws, and the peace of the church and kingdom, they do address themselves to the civil magistrates, justices, and others concerned, imploring their help and assistance for the prevention or suppression of the same, according to the said late act made and set forth in that behalf.

" Lastly, for the better direction of all those who shall be concerned in the advices given by this letter, I desire you will give out amongst ecclesiastical officers and clergy as many copies of the same, as you shall think most conducible to the ends for which it is designed.

" And now, what the success will be, we must leave to God Almighty. Yet I have this confidence under God, that if we do our parts now at first diligently, by God's help and the assistance of the civil power (considering the abundant care and provisions this act contains for our advantages) we shall within a few months see so great an alteration in the distractions of these times, as that the seduced people returning from their seditious and self-serving teachers to the unity of the church, and uniformity in God's service, it will be the glory of God, the welfare of the church, the praise of his majesty's government, and the happiness of the whole kingdom. And so I bid you heartily farewell, and am,—Your most affectionate friend, Gilb. Cant.

"Lambeth house,
May 7, MDCLXX."

(iii) The third letter is taken from the Tanner MSS., vol. cclxxxii. p. 102. It has the title—

"The archbishop of Canterbury's circular letter to cathedrals, that the residentiaries should in their own persons perform divine service on Sundays and holidays at least." [1]

"Right reverend and my very good lord. I have thought this a fit time to give your lordship, and all the rest of my brethren, the bishops of my province, notice of some things, which within some of our own cathedrals, and in the service of God there, are not so orderly performed as they ought to be. Our cathedrals are the standard and rule to all parochial churches of the solemnity

[1] *Ex MS. penes Thom. episc. Assaven.*

and decent manner of reading the liturgy, and
administering the holy sacraments.   And certainly there is none in those places, whom it
better becomes to shew a good example, than
those who have the chief preferments within
those cathedrals ; that is, the deans, canons, prebendaries, and other dignitaries within the same.
But with some trouble I must needs tell you, I
have from many places heard, that the duties of
reading the church service, and administering the
holy communion, have been too much neglected
by those dignified persons ; and as if it were an
office below them, left for the most part to be
performed by their vicars, or petty canons, to the
offence of some of our friends, the advantage of
sectaries, and their own just reproach.   Upon
this, my lord, my advice is, and I do hereby
desire your lordship, that you will call before you
the dean, and canons, or prebendaries of your
cathedral churches, or as many as conveniently
you can get together, and having imparted this
my letter unto them, that your lordship will, as
well in mine as your own name, counsel, and
persuade, or otherwise require them, that they
take care, as much as may be, that divine service,
and administering the holy communion be celebrated by one of themselves, at least every Sunday and holiday in the year ; and that they order
their residence and attendance on the church, so
as (if possible) one of them in person may officiate,
as is before desired.   This, I am assured, will be

very agreeable to his majesty's good pleasure,
conducible to the honour of God's service, and
their own esteem and reputation. And so ex-
pecting from your lordship and them an account
of what is done hereupon, as soon as conveniently
it may be, at least within three months after the
date hereof, I bid your lordship heartily farewell,
and am,—(My lord) your lordship's very affectionate friend and brother, GILB. CANT.

"LAMBETH HOUSE,
June 4, MDCLXX.

"*For the right reverend father in God, my very
good lord and brother, Seth lord bishop of
Sarum.*"

CHAPTER VI

SHELDON AND CHARLES THE SECOND

King Charles the Second's exile—His attitude towards religion—
His character—Clarendon's failure to restrain the King—
Charles' evil life—Sheldon's reproof of King Charles—The
Duke of Richmond's matter—The King refused the Holy
Communion by Sheldon—Sheldon's loss of royal favour in
consequence—Bishop Ken withstands Charles II—Prayer for
Parliament and its reference to King Charles as "most re-
ligious"—Evil influence of the Court upon society—The Duke
of Buckingham—John Evelyn's testimony to the King's loose
morals—Death of Charles II—His neglect of opportunities.

CHARLES STUART was a man of thirty, when he
returned to occupy the throne in 1660. For
fourteen years he had been a wandering exile,
'the penniless guest of many unwilling hosts'
in Holland, France, and Germany. With the exception of a little more than twelve months, passed
in no great comfort in the camp of the Scottish
Covenanters, none of the days of his manhood
had been spent in England. He was in fact
practically a foreigner in thought, habits, and
manner. A man of many parts, endowed with
great natural talents, "a prince of many virtues

and many great imperfections," as Evelyn,[1] who
was much at Court, describes him, he was nevertheless the most consummate and accomplished
of idlers. The practical Pepys confessed that
'the King do mind nothing but pleasures, and
hates the very sight or thoughts of business.'
For if Charles the Second was in earnest about
anything, which is exceedingly doubtful, it was
about his pleasures, and that only.

" His temper was pleasant and social, his
manners perfect, and there was a careless freedom and courtesy in his address which won over
everybody who came into his presence. His
education indeed had been so grossly neglected,
that he could hardly read a plain Latin book.
His shrewdness and vivacity showed itself most
in his endless talk."[2]

The King's morals were of the loosest order,
in keeping with those of the French Court: he
made sport of honourable dealing between man
and man, and he scoffed at purity in women.
Grossly selfish, undisciplined and miserably ungrateful, his personal moral character was simply
despicable. If he had any religious principles
at all, which may reasonably be doubted, they

[1] *Diary*, Feb. 4, 1685.
[2] J. R. Green, *A Short Hist. of the English People*, Lond., 1903,
III, 1353.

lay in the direction of Romanism. So loosely did he sit to religion, that, during his fourteen months' residence in Scotland, he had conformed to the presbyterian forms; and now, in turn, on his return to England he was quite ready to face about and to assume the pose of an enthusiastic Anglican. King Charles' religious frivolity is well illustrated by the fact that even on his death-bed he turned his eyes to his weeping courtiers, and uttered an apology for taking such an unconscionable time in dying!

Charles, though destitute of personal beauty—his features were thin and harsh, his nose large, his lips thick and sensuous—had an affable address, a lively wit, and easy manners. Supple and suave, he had the faculty of making himself exceedingly agreeable amongst any company. He had that careless good humour which so frequently accompanies selfishness and lack of consideration for others. His character was too light and easy to make him either a good lover or a good hater. He was quite prepared to " take to himself any allies who might appear, and to sell himself to any bidder whose terms were high enough." [1] Such was the man, whom, in 1660, the English nation welcomed with open arms and

---

[1] Oman, *Hist. of England*, 19th ed., xxix. 420, 421.

a perfect frenzy of joy! We stand amazed; and yet, sad to say, worse things were to come.

On return to power and position, King Charles II proceeded to develop his unworthy and abominable personal habits without remonstrance. Clarendon, the chief minister of the realm, exerted no influence for good over his royal master. This was Clarendon's great fault. The King filled the royal palace with disreputable profligates and abandoned women. His wife, Catherine of Portugal, was cruelly neglected. Burnet says: " The King was grown very weary of the Queen; and it was believed he had a great mind to be rid of her." [1] Charles permitted his Court to be taken possession of by 'a perfect harem of mistresses,' whose sons he made dukes and earls. Concubine followed concubine in hateful sequence, and the guilt of a troop of profligate women was proclaimed to the world by the gifts of titles and estates to them and their bastard sons. Mr. J. R. Green says—

" The royal bastards were set amongst English nobles. The ducal house of Grafton springs from the King's adultery with Barbara Palmer, whom he created Duchess of Cleveland. The Dukes of St. Albans owe their origin to his

[1] Burnet, *Hist. of his own Time*, London, 1766, vol. i. p. 353.

intrigue with Nell Gwynn, a player and a cour-
tezan.   Louise de Quèrouaille, a mistress sent
by France to win him to its interests, became
Duchess of Portsmouth and ancestress of the
house of Richmond.   An earlier mistress, Lucy
Walters, was mother of a boy whom he raised to
the Dukedom of Monmouth, and to whom the
Dukes of Buccleuch trace their line ; but there is
a good reason for doubting whether the King was
actually his father.   But Charles was far from
being content with these recognised mistresses,
or with a single form of self-indulgence.   Gambling and drinking helped to fill up the vacant
moments when he could no longer toy with his
favourites or bet at Newmarket.   No thought
of remorse or of shame seems ever to have
crossed his mind. . . . From shame indeed he
was shielded by his cynical disbelief in human
virtue." [1]

Never before had England been put to shame
so thoroughly by open immorality in high places.
How the nation stood it all, simply amazes us.

"The King's companions and servants were,
as might have been expected, men of scandalous
life, and quite unfit for the offices into which he
thrust them.   The tone of the court had a profound and unhappy influence on the manners of
the day.   Never were the private vices dis-

---

[1] J. R. Green, *A Short Hist. of the English People*, III.,
1353 ff.

played so unblushingly. . . . England plunged into extravagance and evil living of all sorts. Drunkenness, profanity, thriftless luxury, gambling, duelling, shameless lust, were accounted no discredit. The literature, and more especially the drama, of the Restoration is coarse and foul beyond belief. . . . The days of the great civil war had brought out the sterner virtues of Englishmen; the Restoration and the reign of domestic peace were marked by the outburst of all the folly and lewd frivolity which had so long been dormant beneath the surface." [1]

This is a terrible and tremendous indictment, true to the letter. The person to whom this appalling state of immorality was primarily and mainly due—the person who, in God's sight, was directly responsible in largest measure — was Charles Stuart, the restored monarch, Charles II. And, be it carefully noted, the man who dared to remonstrate with and reprove the abandoned and profligate King was Gilbert Sheldon, as we are now to see.

To his eternal honour, Sheldon stands out prominently against a dark background of hideous immorality and foulness, as the man with clean hands and a pure heart, who had thus the right and the moral courage to rebuke the iniquities of

[1] Oman, *Hist. of England*, 19th ed., xxix. 425, 426.

King Charles the Second and his degraded Court
—as the man who had the heroic courage to
speak out, and take the consequences. As the
prophet Elijah before King Ahab, and as St. John
the Baptist before King Herod, Gilbert Sheldon
confronted King Charles, and bade him in God's
name purge his own life and his Court from the
plague.

As to what exactly passed between the Archbishop and the King on this memorable occasion
we do not precisely know, and probably never
shall know. From Pepys, as will be seen later,
there was evidently 'a scene.' Bishop Burnet
gives some information upon the point in regard
to King Charles and the Duchess of Richmond—

" Mistress Steward," [1] as he spells the surname,
" had gained so much on the King, and yet kept
her ground with so much firmness, that the King
seemed to design if possible to legitimate his
addresses to her, when he saw no hope of succeeding any other way. The Duke of Richmond,
being a widower, courted her. The King seemed
to give way to it; and pretended to take such
care of her, that he would have good settlements
made for her. He hoped by that means to have

[1] Mrs. Frances Stuart, afterwards Duchess of Richmond, a
reputed mistress of King Charles II. See Burnet, *Hist. of his own
Time*, London, 1766, vol. ii. p. 212, vol. iii. p. 427.

broke the matter decently. Lord Clarendon was afraid lest strange methods should be taken to get rid of the Queen, and to make way for her. When the King saw that she had a mind to marry the Duke of Richmond, he offered to make her a Duchess, and to settle an estate upon her. Upon this she said, she saw she must either marry him, or suffer much in the opinion of the world." [1]

The lady later married the Duke privately, and without acquainting the King, who was greatly enraged. Burnet speaks of his Majesty as 'one in rage that forgot all decency,' who was 'full of fury.' Blaming Lord Clarendon in the matter of the marriage of the Duke with Mrs. Stewart, he resolved to remove Lord Clarendon from office. Whereupon, Burnet resumes :—

"As soon as it was done, the King sent for Sheldon, and told him what he had done. But he answered nothing. When the King insisted to oblige him to declare himself, Sheldon said, 'Sir, I wish you would put away this woman that you keep.' The King upon that replied sharply, why he had never talked to him of that sooner, but took this occasion now to speak of it. Lauderdale told me he had all this from the King : and that the King and Sheldon had gone

---

[1] Burnet, *Hist. of his own Time*, vol. i. pp. 353 ff.

into such expostulations upon it, that from that day forward Sheldon could never recover the King's confidence."

Swift, in his notes in a later edition of Burnet's *History of his Own Time*, tells us that Sheldon " refused the Sacrament to the King" on account of his shameless adultery.[1] This took place in 1667. To this transaction, in which Sheldon played so fine and admirable a part, somewhat obscured by the historians of the period, Samuel Pepys refers in his *Diary and Correspondence*[2] as follows—

" The Duke of York tells me that the business of getting the Duchess of Richmond to Court is broke off, her husband not suffering it; and thereby great trouble is brought among the people that endeavoured it, and thought they had compassed it. And, Lord! to think that at this time the King should mind no other cares but these! He tells me that my Lord of Canterbury (Sheldon) is a mighty stout man, and a man of brave, high spirit, and cares not for this disfavour that he is under at Court, knowing that the King cannot take away his profits during his life, and therefore do not value it."

[1] Burnet, *History of his own Time*, vol. i. p. 355. For Swift's account, see later in these pages.
[2] Lond., 1877, vol. v. pp. 133, 134, under December 27, 1667; see also p. 132.

Pepys might well have omitted his allusion to possible financial loss—a thing which Sheldon, in whose heart the love of money had no place, was not likely to consider in doing his duty. That the royal displeasure of such a profligate king as Charles Stuart should cost him any regret, is inconceivable. Sheldon was content to do that which his conscience bade him do, and to ignore consequences. This must ever remain the true ideal of duty—to do the thing that is right, reckless of results to oneself. We can readily form some idea of what it cost him to bear his righteous witness, for we learn from Pepys the high esteem in which Charles II held Sheldon, and which had led the King to designate him for the Bishopric of London, and later for the Archbishopric of Canterbury—

"The Bishop of London is now (September 1662) one of the most powerful men in England with the King." "For (May 1663) aught I hear, the Bishopp of London keeps as great with the King as ever."[1]

Gilbert Sheldon's courageous rebuke of Charles II is only equalled by that of Thomas Ken (Bishop of Bath and Wells at a later date), who

[1] Vol. ii. pp. 38, 209.

bravely withstood King Charles in the matter of one of his many mistresses, Nell Gwynn.[1] It is said that

"upon the removal of the Court to pass the summer at Winchester, the doctor's (Ken's) prebendal house was pitched upon for the use of Mrs. Eleanor Gwyn. But Ken was too pious even to countenance vice in his royal benefactor; and therefore positively refused admittance to the royal mistress, which the King, however, did not take amiss, as he knew the sincerity of the man; and previous to any application, nominated him soon after to the bishopric of Bath and Wells."[2]

In the case of Sheldon, no recognition of fidelity to duty followed at the hands of the sovereign he strove to save.

In 1661, when the Prayer Book was revised,

"a new collect was also drawn for the Parliament, in which a new epithet was added to the King's title, that gave great offence, and occasioned much indecent raillery: He was styled our most religious King. It was not easy to give a proper sense to this, and to make it go well down; since, whatever the signification of religion might be in the Latin word, as importing the sacredness of

[1] Mother of the Duke of St. Albans, who early in life achieved a high reputation.

[2] Chalmers, *General Biographical Dict.*, Lond., 1815, vol. xix. p. 300.

the King's person, yet in the English language it bore a signification that was no way applicable to the King. And those who took great liberties with him have often asked him, what must all his people think, when they heard him prayed for as their most religious King?"[1]

In speaking of this, an eminent liturgical scholar of our own day, the late Dr. Dowden, once Bishop of Edinburgh, says—

"In the *Prayer for the High Court of Parliament* the epithets, 'most religious and gracious,' as applied to the Sovereign, have at various times given rise to cavil. The attempt made to defend the term 'most religious,' on the ground that 'religious' was in old English used as expressive of attention to the *outward forms* of religion, is unavailing in the face of the fact that even the outward forms have had scant consideration from some English sovereigns to whom the words were applied. Nor can I accept the apology that some of the Eastern Liturgies exbibit language equally laudatory of the emperors. The words in our English prayer may have been really not unsuitable when first used of Charles I in occasional forms put out in 1625 and 1628. But it was indeed unfortunate that the Prayer Book of the Church of England should have adopted such language with reference to his

[1] Burnet, *Hist. of his own Time*, Lond., 1766, vol. i. p. 256.

K

profligate son, Charles II. In the great outburst of loyalty at the Restoration, and probably in ignorance of the real character of the young king, it was not unnatural that a form which was ready at hand should be incorporated for permanent use in the Prayer Book. But the complete shifting of the sense of the word ' religious' has made the term as thus applied a mockery during the reigns of too many of our sovereigns."[1]

As an instance and by way of example of what the influence of the Court of Charles II had upon society, we may mention that an historian of eminence has recorded that—

"the truest type of the time (of the Restoration) is the Duke of Buckingham, and the most characteristic event in the Duke's life was a duel in which he consummated his seduction of Lady Shrewsbury by killing her husband, while the Countess in disguise as a page held his horse for him and looked on at the murder."[2]

It is some small consolation to gather from the memoirs of the period that the more abominable and violent forms of vice were practically confined to London and the Court. The Restoration was

[1] Dowden, *The Workmanship of the Prayer Book*, 2nd ed., pp. 221, 222.
[2] J. R. Green, *A Short Hist. of the English People*, Lond., 1874, ch. ix. p. 589.

a time of "wickedness in high places," practised openly and shamelessly by those who knew better: and God again left not Himself without witness in the person of His servant Gilbert Sheldon.

As to how completely Charles the Second disregarded Archbishop Sheldon's remonstrance and protest, the following quotations from Evelyn show—

1684, Christmas Day—"Decr 25th Dr. Dove preached before the King. I saw this evening such a scene of profuse gaming, and the King in the midst of his three concubines, as I had never before seen—luxurious dallying and profaneness."

Under Feb. 4, 1685—

"I can never forget the inexpressible luxury and profaneness, gaming, and all dissoluteness, and as it were total forgetfulness of God, (it being Sunday evening), which this day se'nnight I was witness of, the King sitting and toying with his concubines, Portsmouth, Cleveland, and Mazarine, etc., a French boy singing love-songs, in that glorious gallery, whilst about twenty of the great courtiers and other dissolute persons were at Basset round a large table, a bank of at least 2000 in gold before them; upon which two gentlemen who were with me made reflections with astonishment.   Six days after was all in the dust!"[1]

King Charles the Second passed to his account on February 6, 1685—a monument of a high vocation refused, of solemn warnings disregarded, of splendid opportunities wasted; in vivid contrast to the conduct and career of the great Archbishop who strenuously strove to save him from moral ruin, and to guide him to fulfil his high destiny.

"Never had King," wrote John Evelyn, who knew him well, "more glorious opportunities to have made himself, his people, and all Europe happy, and prevented innumerable mischiefs, had not his too easy nature resigned him to be managed by crafty men, and some abandoned and profaned wretches who corrupted his otherwise sufficient parts, disciplined as he had been by many afflictions during his banishment, which gave him much experience and knowledge of men and things; but those wicked creatures took him off from all application becoming so great a King. . . . He was ever kind to me, and very gracious upon all occasions."[2]

[1] *Diary and Correspondence of John Evelyn*, Lond., 1850, vol. ii. pp. 203, 210.
[2] *Ibid.*, vol. ii. p. 207.

CHAPTER VII

THE SHELDONIAN THEATRE

The Sheldonian Theatre, Oxford, Sheldon's memorial—Its cost
—Sir Christopher Wren, the architect—At first contained
the University Press—Evelyn's visit to the Theatre—The
Encaenia observed in the Theatre in 1669—Evelyn's descrip-
tion thereof—The Theatre described—The Sheldonian Press
—Sheldon's letters—His Bible.

In Oxford Archbishop Sheldon's name and
memory are perpetuated in the Sheldonian
Theatre, which is so named after him. It was
built at his sole expense, costing £25,000, from
the designs of Sir Christopher Wren, and opened
in A.D. 1669. When Sheldon had disposed of
the mass of business connected with the reorganisation of the Church, with characteristic
energy he put his mind into this great under-
taking. The Sheldonian Theatre was the great
architect's first work, and laid an enduring foundation for his future fame. On the completion
of the building, Archbishop Sheldon presented
Wren with a golden cup. The annual Act or

"Encaenia," a commemoration of benefactors, accompanied by the recitation of prize compositions and the conferment of honorary degrees, has almost invariably been held in this building. From 1669 to 1713 it contained the University Press:[1] at the latter date the Clarendon Building,[2] a prominent object in Broad Street, was erected to accommodate the growing establishment, which was ultimately moved in 1830 to the present Clarendon Press.

---

[1] "A.D. 1674. In this year appeared the third *Catalogus impressorum Librorum Bibliothecæ Bodleianæ*, in one folio volume, divided into two parts of 478 and 272 pages respectively. It is dedicated to Archbishop Sheldon, by Hyde the librarian, not without reason, as being printed in that Theatre which the Archbishop had so lately built."—Macray, *Annals of the Bodleian Library*, Oxford, 1868, p. 97. The dedication is surmounted with a headpiece containing the arms of the See of Canterbury, over which is a mitre, and runs—"Reverendissimo in Christo Patri ac Domino D. GILBERTO providentia divina Archiepiscopo Cautuariensi, totius Angliæ Primati et Metropolitani."

[2] The Old Clarendon Printing Office was erected by Sir John Vanburgh from the profits of the sale of Clarendon's *History of the Rebellion*, given exclusively and for ever to the University by the son of the author.

"In the exercise of his office, as Curator of the Theatre, Gardiner transferred the University Press from the Theatre to the newly-erected Clarendon Buildings, and, being also Vice-Chancellor (1712–1715), was responsible for substituting the name Clarendon for that of Sheldon, 'the true benefactor of Oxford printing.' No one, we may be sure, would have rejoiced more than Sheldon that the name of Clarendon should be perpetuated in the stately buildings erected out of the profits of the 'History of the Great Rebellion,' and that his own undoubted claims to be the father of the Oxford Press should be forgotten in favour of his dearest friend."—Burrows, *Worthies of All Souls*, pp. 369, 370.

THE SHELDONIAN THEATRE
From an old engraving

John Evelyn, writing in the year 1664 (October 24), speaks of visiting

"the new Theatre, now building at an exceeding and royal expense by the Lord Archbishop of Canterbury [Sheldon], to keep the Acts in for the future, till now being in St. Mary's church."

He goes on to say—

"The foundation had been newly laid, and the whole designed by that incomparable genius, my worthy friend, Dr. Christopher Wren, who showed me the model, not disdaining my advice in some particulars."[1]

Evelyn was in Oxford in 1669, and on July 9 of that year was present at the Encaenia in the Sheldonian Theatre : he writes—[2]

"A.D. 1669, July 9—In the morning, was celebrated the Encaenia of the New Theatre, so magnificently built by the munificence of Dr. Gilbert Sheldon, Archbishop of Canterbury, in which was spent £25,000, as Sir Christopher Wren, the architect (as I remember) told me ; and yet it was never seen by the benefactor, my Lord Archbishop having told me that he

[1] *Diary and Correspondence of John Evelyn, F.R.S.* ; ed. Bray, Lond., 1850, vol. i. p. 384.
[2] *Ibid.*, vol. ii. pp. 39, 40.

never did nor ever would see it. It is, in truth, a fabric comparable to any of this kind of former ages, and doubtless exceeding any of the present, as this University does for colleges, libraries, schools, students and order, all the Universities in the world. To the theatre is added the famous Sheldonian printing-house. This being at the Act and the first time of opening the Theatre (Acts being formerly kept in St. Mary's Church, which might be thought indecent, that being a place set apart for the immediate worship of God, and was the inducement for building this noble pile), it was now resolved to keep the present Act in it, and celebrate its dedication with the greatest splendour and formality that might be ; and, therefore, draw a world of strangers, and other company, to the University, from all parts of the nation.

" The Vice-Chancellor, Heads of Houses, and Doctors, being seated in magisterial seats, the Vice-Chancellor's chair and desks, Proctors, etc.; covered with brocatelle (a kind of brocade) and cloth of gold ; the University Registrar read the founder's grant and gift of it to the University for their scholastic exercises upon these solemn occasions. Then followed Dr. South, the University's orator, in an eloquent speech, which was very long, and not without some malicious and indecent reflections on the Royal Society, as underminers of the University ; which was very foolish and untrue, as well as unreasonable . . . the rest was in praise of the Archbishop and the ingenious architect. This ended, after loud music from the corridor above, where an organ was placed, there followed divers panegyric speeches. . . . This lasted from eleven in the morning till seven at night, which was concluded with ringing of bells, and universal joy and feasting. The next day, began the more solemn lectures in all the faculties, which were performed in their several schools. . . . The assembly now returned to the Theatre, where the *Terræ filius* (the *University Buffoon* [1]) entertained the auditory with a tedious, abusive, sarcastical rhapsody, most unbecoming the gravity of the University, and that so grossly, that unless it be suppressed, it will be of ill consequence, as I afterwards plainly expressed my sense of it both to the Vice-Chancellor and several Heads of Houses, who were perfectly ashamed of it, and resolved to take care of it in future. After this ribaldry, the Proctors made their speeches. . . . Last of all, the Vice-Chancellor, shutting up the whole in a panegyrical oration, celebrating their benefactor and the rest, apposite to the occasion. Then was the Theatre dedicated by the scholastic exercises in all the Faculties with great solemnity." [2]

In architecture the Sheldonian Theatre is an imitation of ancient theatres, specially that of

[1] An imitation of the mediæval Jesters : the origin of the title is not known.

[2] *Diary and Correspondence of John Evelyn*, vol. ii. pp. 39 ff.

Marcellus at Rome. The iron railing in front of it is varied by colossal heads, but it is not known whom they are intended to represent. The internal measurements are 80 feet by 70 feet; the roof is flat, of ingenious geometrical construction, designed to represent a canvas stretched over gilt cordage. This is arranged in view of the fact that the ancient classic theatres were roofless, and open to the sky. The roof was painted by Streater, Sergeant-Painter to Charles II. The Sheldonian Theatre is capable of holding over 3000 persons, and it is considered to be one of the finest rooms for public purposes possessed by any public body in Europe. The Sheldonian Press is famous for producing some magnificent specimens of typography and steel engraving— work which may perhaps be rarely equalled in the present day, but not beaten. The justice of this opinion will become evident to anyone who is able to examine, for example, the beautiful letterpress and steel engravings of such works as the *Catalogus impressorum librorum Bibliothecæ Bodleianæ in Academia Oxoniensi, Oxonii, e Theatro Sheldoniano* MDCLXXIV; or the *Historia et Antiquitates Universitatis Oxoniensis*, and its companion volume, *Oxonia Illustrata*, issued by the same Press, MDCLXXIV–V., to which refer-

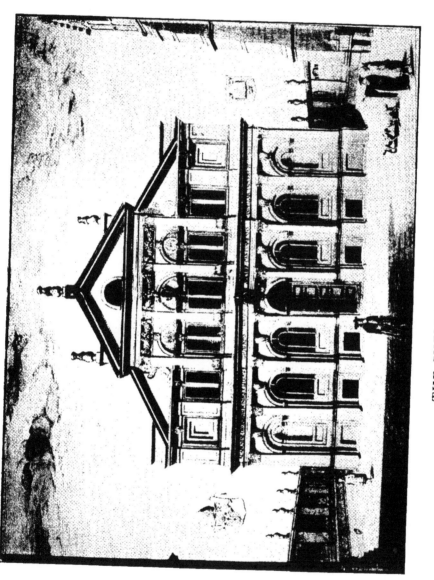

THE SHELDONIAN THEATRE
From an old engraving

ence is made elsewhere in the present work. For a contemporary account of the Sheldonian Theatre, the work named second in order above should be consulted.[1]

"A.D. 1824. A collection of valuable original papers relating to affairs in Church and State, which had belonged to Archbishop Sheldon, were sold by his great-nephew, Sir John English Dolben, of Finedon, Northamptonshire, to the (Bodleian) Library for £40, 5s. They are now bound in six volumes, of which three are lettered *Sheldon*, and three *Dolben*. Of the first three, two contain letters from English, Welsh, Scotch (*sic*) and Irish Bishops, and the contents of the other are miscellaneous; of the second three, one contains miscellaneous letters and papers commencing at 1585, another has similar papers from 1626 to 1721, and the third contains miscellaneous ecclesiastical letters and documents. Some of the letters are addressed to the Archbishop's secretary, Miles Smyth, Esq. A short letter from Sir John Dolben to Dr. Bandinel, relating to his disposal of these papers, dated Oct. 12, 1824, is preserved in Bodl. MS. Addit. ii. A. 32. He had previously given, in 1822, a fine copy of a quarto Bible which had belonged to Sheldon, containing (1) the Prayer-Book and Metrical Psalms, printed at Cambridge in 1638, (2) the Old Test., printed by Field at London in 1648, and (3) the New

---

[1] *Hist. et Antiq.*, lib. ii., foll. 25 ff.

Test., Cambr. 1637. At the end are some memoranda by the Archbishop of the births, baptisms, and deaths of members of the Sheldon and Okeover families, and of the legitimate children of Charles II and the Duke of York."
—Macray, *Annals of the Bodleian Library, Oxford*, 1868, p. 237.

CHAPTER VIII

THE PLAGUE AND THE GREAT FIRE: SAINT PAUL'S CATHEDRAL: LONDON HOUSE: LAMBETH PALACE LIBRARY

The Great Plague of London—Sheldon remains at Lambeth ministering to the plague-stricken people—Burnet's silence concerning Sheldon's courage and fidelity—The Great Fire of London—Results of the conflagration—Old Saint Paul's Cathedral destroyed—John Evelyn's description of the fire—Description of Old Saint Paul's—Inigo Jones's portico—Sheldon's munificence to both Old and New Saint Paul's—His influence in the appointment of Wren as architect of New Saint Paul's—Sheldon's letter in reference to the collection of funds—Laud's legacy—The rebuilding of Saint Paul's—Its dimensions—Ungrateful treatment of Wren—His tomb—Sheldon's gift of London House to the See of London—Some account of London House—Lambeth Library—Sheldon's restoration of the Library premises—Late date of the style "Lambeth Palace"—Statement of the gifts of Gilbert Sheldon.

IN the second year of Archbishop Sheldon's tenure of the primacy (A.D. 1665), the land was visited by the most awful and deadly pestilence ever experienced. In London the Great Plague raged with terrible fury. Sanitary arrangements were practically unknown; the city was badly built and overcrowded, and, filthy beyond description, it became a veritable hot-bed of infection and contagion. Death and desertion, sweeping along through streets and districts, carried thousands to their doom. Clergy and doctors of medicine fled for safety into the country. Late in the autumn of 1665 the metropolis wore the aspect of a city of the dead, and grass was growing thick and high in the streets. Hard by St. Martin's-in-the-Fields and at Mile End huge pits had been filled with corpses as fast as they could be dug, with huddled bodies collected in the dismal and dreaded death-carts. It is estimated that about 100,000 inhabitants perished in the pestilence.

When almost everyone who could had fled from the terrors of the doomed city, Gilbert Sheldon, true to his consecration vow,[1] with heroic courage, remained faithfully at his post. Not only did he never leave Lambeth, though victims were dying in numbers at the very gates of the palace, but he ministered to their needs of his own wealth. By his letters to the bishops and others, he collected considerable

---

[1] "Will you shew yourself gentle, and be merciful for Christ's sake to poor and needy people, and to all strangers destitute of help?" "I will so shew myself by God's help."—*Form of Consecrating a Bishop:* B. of C. P.

sums of money for the benefit of the sufferers from all parts of his Province. Echard says:—

"Archbishop Sheldon firmly continued all the time of the greatest danger, and with his diffusive charity preserved great numbers alive that would have perished in their necessities, and by his affecting letters to all the Bishops procured great sums to be returned out of all parts of his Province."[1]

Burnet, always the detractor of Sheldon, in mentioning the Great Plague, is strangely silent as to the Archbishop's splendid heroism and self-sacrifice, which must certainly have made a deep impression at the time, and done the English Church an immense amount of good at a critical period in its history. Sheldon seized the golden opportunity, and showed the martyr-spirit, and undoubtedly gained such an influence as few men of the time acquired: for the majority of the clergy who fled the doomed city were branded with the mask of self-seeking and cowardice, which must have lessened their influence immensely on returning to their parishes when the danger had passed away. Anyhow it served to exhibit the kind of metal of which Sheldon was made, for it is always in the last resort, in

[1] Echard, *Hist. of England*, vol. iii. p. 142.

the face of personal danger, that the true character of a man emerges.

The summer of the year 1666 had been the dryest known for some years. London, being for the most part built of timber filled in with plaster, to use Burnet's description, " all was extream dry." The wooden houses, as dry as tinder, were ready for the impending calamity. A baker's oven in Pudding Lane, near Fleet Street Hill and ·Eastcheap, caught fire on a sultry night : it was windward, in the prevailing easterly winds, to the heart of the city. This happened at midnight between September 1 and 2. For five days and nights the fire raged, and London as a city was practically obliterated. The result of the conflagration has been stated to be as follows : 396 acres of houses were gutted, 400 streets, 13,200 dwelling-houses, 89 churches, besides chapels, 4 of the city-gates, the Exchange, the Custom House, part of the Guildhall, and most of the city companies' halls, and other stately buildings of all kinds, alike perished.[1]

The extent of the ruin is absolutely unparalleled : the earthquake of Lisbon, in that

[1] See Loftie, *Hist. of London*, 1883, vol. i. p. 360.

OLD ST. PAUL'S CATHEDRAL (WITH THE SPIRE)

London was so much greater, was as nothing in comparison.

The Great Fire, following hard on the heels of the Great Plague, was providential, for it wiped out for ever hundreds of fever-dens, and permitted the reconstruction of the city with wider thoroughfares and more direct communications. It is a matter for extreme regret, however, that almost all the great and historical buildings of mediæval London perished in the conflagration—the historic mansions of the nobility, the halls of the wealthy city companies, the Guildhall, some ninety churches, and, in particular, the old Gothic Cathedral Church of St. Paul.

In his *Diary*, under September 7, 1666, John Evelyn relates :—

" I went this morning on foot from Whitehall as far as London Bridge. . . . At my return, I was infinitely concerned to find that goodly Church, St. Paul's, now a sad ruin, and that beautiful portico now rent in pieces, flakes of stone split asunder, and nothing remaining entire but the inscription[1] in the architrave, showing by whom it was built, which had not one letter defaced ! It was astonishing to see what immense stones the heat had in a manner calcined, so that

[1] Carolus. D. G. Magnæ Britanniæ, Franciæ, Hib. Rex Templū Divi Pauli vetustate consūptū restitute Porticū *adjecit*.

all the ornaments, columns, friezes, capitals, and projectures of massy Portland stone, flew off, even to the very roof, where a sheet of lead covering a great space (not less than six acres by measure) was totally melted; the ruins of the vaulted roof falling, broke into St. Faith's, which being filled with magazines of books belonging to the Stationers, and being carried thither for safety, they were all consumed, burning for a week following. . . . Thus lay in ashes that most venerable church, one of the most ancient pieces of early piety in the Christian world."[1]

We can readily imagine the dismay which must have filled the mind of Archbishop Sheldon as he witnessed from Lambeth, or heard elsewhere the news of, this terrible havoc and destruction which befell the churches of the city. The burning of old St. Paul's alone would be in his eyes an irreparable catastrophe, for, when Bishop of London, he had been foremost in contributing munificently to the scheme on foot for its restoration the sum of over £2000.[2] The old cathedral, like the Abbey of St. Albans, was remarkable for its vast dimensions. The nave was Norman, having twelve bays, and had been at first roofed

---

[1] *Diary of John Evelyn*, London, 1850, vol. ii. pp. 13, 14.
[2] The precise sum appears to have been £2169, 17s. 10d., representing more than £10,000 of our money to-day.

with flat timbers, until probably in the fifteenth century it had been vaulted above the Early English clerestory, as shown in Hollar's plate of A.D. 1658, given in Dugdale's *History of St. Paul's.* The tower, placed at the crossing of nave and choir, had large windows shedding light into the juncture of the transepts. The spire surmounting the tower, the loftiest in Christendom, must have presented a magnificent appearance; for, according to a contemporary authority, it rose to the amazing height of 520 feet:[1] but being of wood and unprotected by lightning conductors, it had been struck by lightning in 1444 and partially consumed by fire; only in turn, after being rebuilt in 1561, to be wholly destroyed. No attempt was then made to rebuild it. The old cathedral had no western towers, until Inigo Jones, under the patronage of King James I in 1633, commenced some restoration and addition. At the expense of King Charles I, Inigo Jones had the audacity and bad taste to attach a classic portico to the old Gothic church. This portico, 200 feet long, 40 feet high, and 50 feet deep, is shown in Hollar's plate of 1656; and Jones built two small

---

[1] This wooden spire was surmounted by a cross, the staff of which was 15 feet in height, and the cross beam 6 feet in length.

towers behind his incongruous portico.[1]   The choir was separated from the nave by a lofty screen of stone; its architecture, like that of the transepts, was Decorated.   The east end of the choir was crowned by a lofty Lady Chapel, with an exceedingly elaborate and beautiful rose window.

Such was this glorious cathedral church of the Metropolis before the Great Fire in 1666, to the repair and restoration of which Gilbert Sheldon contributed so largely.   The necessity of this repair and restoration had become more urgent in his time, for the Puritans, who regarded St. Paul's as too vast for preaching purposes, had considerably injured the whole structure, as their manner was, and the new portico of Inigo Jones in particular, permitting booths to be erected in it.   Stow says, "The body of the church was converted to a Horse - Guard for troopers to quarter in."[2]   The epitaph of a dean, who died in 1664, had its peculiar significance—"Among

[1] For a full description of old St. Paul's, see Stow, *Survey*, 6th ed. vol. i., fol. 646.

For one hundred years the cathedral had been bereft of its ancient peal of bells; for Henry VIII had profanely claimed them as his own, and more sacrilegiously lost them, and the belfry in which they hung, to Sir Miles Partridge at a game of dice!   At that time the belfry stood at the eastern end of St. Paul's Church-yard.   See *ibid.*, fol. 643.

[2] *Survey*, vol. i., fol. 647.

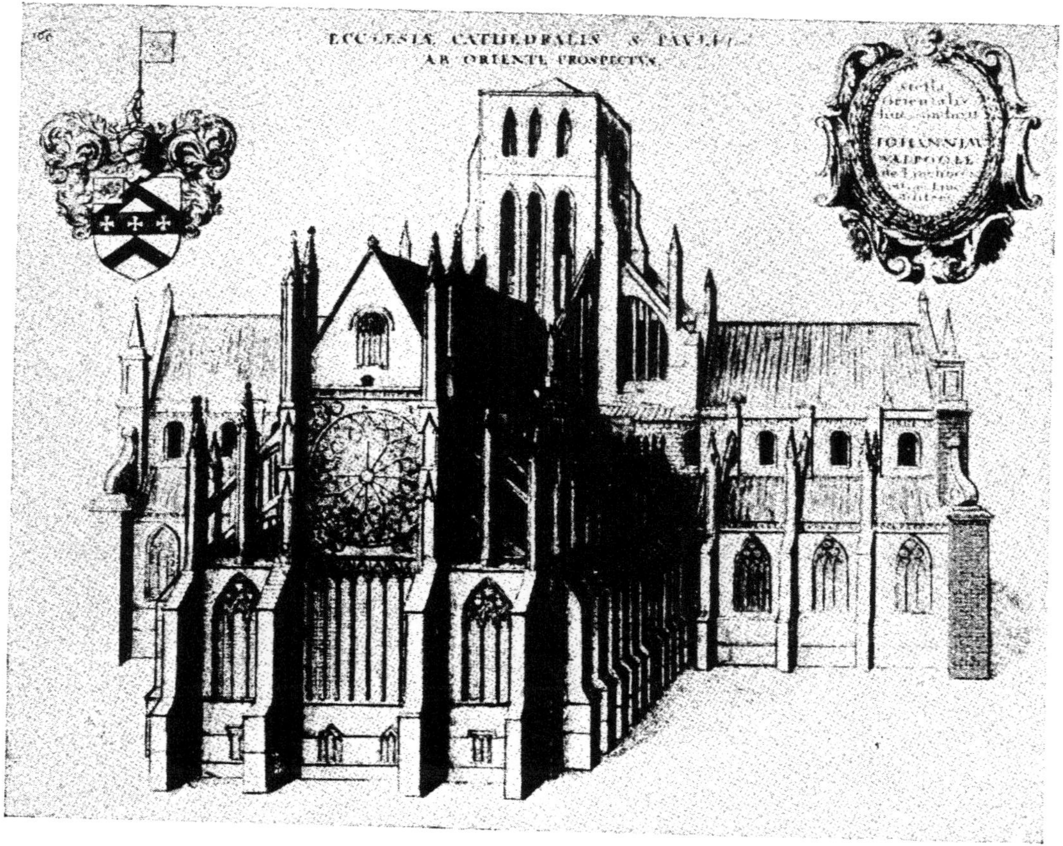
ECCLESIÆ CATHEDRALIS S. PAVLI
AB ORIENTE PROSPECTVS
IOHANNIS
WALPOOLE

OLD ST. PAUL'S CATHEDRAL

these sacred ruins his own are laid, in'the certainty that both shall rise again."[1] Writing of the Great Fire, Dryden[2] has—

> "The daring flames peep'd in, and saw from far
> The awful beauties of the sacred quire :
> But, since it was profan'd by Civil War,
> Heav'n thought it fit to have it purg'd by fire."

To the rebuilding of St. Paul's Archbishop Sheldon was a liberal contributor. Malcolm[3] says, "his subscription to the repair and rebuilding of St. Paul's amounted to £2000"; in our own day this sum must be multiplied by four or five. The architect chosen for this great task was Christopher Wren, son of Dr. Christopher Wren, Rector of Hazeley, Oxon., and Dean of Windsor, and nephew of the Bishop of Ely. During the building of St. Paul's his salary was but £200 a year. It seems highly probable that Sheldon's influence is to be traced in the matter of the choice of Wren as architect of the new cathedral. He was the patron of Wren, and brought him to the front in employing him to design and build the Sheldonian Theatre, which was Wren's first work, and

---

[1] Quoted by Loftie, *Hist. of London*, vol. i. p. 365.
[2] Stanza 29 from end of *Annus Mirabilis*, so called because both Plague and Fire fell within a twelvemonth.
[3] *Londinium Redivivum*, Lond., 1803, vol. iii. p. 90.

made his name. In selecting Wren, then an un-- tried and unknown architect, and permitting him to spend at least £100,000 of our money of to- day, Sheldon proved both his penetration and his munificence. Had Sheldon employed another architect for the Sheldonian Theatre, it is not unlikely that some other name than that of Christopher Wren would have been associated with the new Cathedral of London. When Sheldon was Warden of All Souls, Wren was a Junior Fellow of that College. Thus these two great men were old friends.

On September 14, 1676, the commissioners for rebuilding St. Paul's issued an address, or order, to the bishops, recommending and in- viting contributions from themselves and their several dioceses. The following is Archbishop Sheldon's reply.[1]

"MY VERY GOOD LORD,—I have perused the enclosed order and direction of his majesties commissioners for the rebuilding of St. Paul's, and shall effectually pursue the same within my diocese, and other parts of my jurisdiction; and your lordship shall have a particular amount thereof in some short time.

"By the tenor of the commission, I conceive

[1] Malcolm, *Londinium Redivivum*, Lond., 1803, vol. iii. p. 90.

either your lordship, or other commissioners, most proper to communicate this affayr to the rest of my brethren yᵉ bishops; and rather, because it relates to both provinces; and your lordship is especially thereby entrusted with the return, and the commissioners with the examination of it: but, if my name should be thought necessary, I shall write unto your lordship according to the usual manner, and shall be most ready to contribute what other assistance I can that may conduce either to the execution or expedition of so laudable a designe. In the mean time, I am, my lord, your lordship's very affectionate friend and brother,

"GUILB. CANT.

"CROYDON, *September* 1, 1676."

This letter was written by Sheldon but a year before he died. He had lived only long enough to see the work put in hand, and the first stone laid (June 21, 1675). It is interesting to know that Archbishop Laud left a legacy of £800 towards the repair of old St. Paul's, which was paid over by half-yearly instalments of £200, to the fund for the rebuilding of the cathedral.

It has been said of Wren's predecessor at St. Paul's, Inigo Jones, that he was a man of genius without an opportunity: in the case of Christopher Wren, a great man and a great opportunity happily met. The Great Fire of London, by its wholesale destruction of St. Paul's and all the city churches, gave Wren a scope for his talents, such as probably no other architect ever had to the same extent. Just before the Fire, Charles II had asked Wren to prepare a scheme for the restoration of old St. Paul's. In May 1661 he submitted his report and designs for the work. The old cathedral was in a very ruinous state, as we have already seen, and Wren proposed to remodel the greater part of it, "after the good Roman manner," as he said, and not "to follow the Gothick rudeness of the old design." According to this scheme, only the old choir was to be left; the nave and transepts were to be rebuilt after the classical style, with a lofty dome at the crossing—not unlike the plan which in the new St. Paul's was ultimately carried out. But in 1666, the same year, the Fire occurred. A new design was thus required at Wren's hands, the results of which in its final form are familiar to us. The ground began to be cleared in May 1, 1674; the first stone was laid at the S.E. corner of the choir by Edward Strong, the mason, and the second by Mr. Longland, on June 21, 1675. Service was performed for the first time in the choir of the new cathedral on December 2, 1697; whilst the last stone was laid, in the presence of the great architect, by his son in 1710, thirty years after the laying of the first. The building was commenced and completed under one architect and one master builder, while one Bishop, Dr. Compton, presided over the diocese of London. The total cost, not including later adornments, was close upon £748,000, the major part of which was raised by a tax, imposed by several Acts of Parliament, on every chaldron of coal brought into the port of London.[1] The extreme height of St. Paul's is, from the top of the cross to the pavement, 365 feet; extreme length, 500 feet; width of the transepts, 250 feet; diameter of the dome, externally, 145 feet, internally, 108 feet; interior height of the nave, 80 feet; height of western towers, 222 feet.[2] Any attempt at a detailed account of St. Paul's is not necessary here, but any readers of this volume who may desire further information will find it in Mr. Basil Champneys' article in the *Magazine of Art* of June 1882. The only cathedral church in Europe worthy to be compared with the present St. Paul's is that of St. Peter's, Rome, which, in regard to size, is

[1] See Cunningham, *Handbook of London, Past and Present,* Murray, 1850, p. 382.
[2] See Loftie, *Hist. of London,* vol. i. p. 388.

superior—St. Paul's could actually stand within St. Peter's. For the whole subject of St. Paul's Cathedral, old and new, Mr. William Longman's profusely illustrated work, *A History of the Three Cathedrals dedicated to St. Paul in London*,[1] may with much advantage be studied. It remains to be recorded that Archbishop Sheldon was the first name on the list of the Committee for restoring or rebuilding St. Paul's after the Great Fire.[2]

Wren was subjected to much annoyance in regard to his designs for St. Paul's, and he was not well treated in his old age. In 1718, to their enduring disgrace, King George I and others dismissed Wren by superseding his patent: five years later he died. No one could hope to approach the great architect in genius, and no one tried so to do. His name comes down to us surrounded with its own peculiar fragrance. In his old age he retired to his house in Warwickshire, and from thence it was his wont to visit London once a year, and to sit and reflect for a time under the mighty dome he had built. He died in his ninety-first year, and his body

---

[1] Lond., Longmans, Green, & Co., 1873; with 6 engravings on steel and nearly 50 woodcut illustrations.
[2] *Ibid.* vii. 93.

appropriately rests in the crypt, with the epitaph on his grave—*Si monumentum requiris, circumspice.*[1]

At the extreme east of the crypt, in the south side, on a black marble slab, are inscribed the following simple words :—

HERE LIETH

SIR CHRISTOPHER WREN

THE BUILDER OF THIS CATHEDRAL

CHURCH OF ST. PAUL, &C.,

WHO DYED

IN THE YEAR OF OUR LORD

MDCCXXIII

AND OF HIS AGE XCI.

The inscription, which once appeared in front of the organ gallery, was removed with the gallery, and may now be seen over the door of the north transept.[2]

Amongst Gilbert Sheldon's munificent acts was the purchase from Lord Petre of London House, a handsome brick building on the west side of Aldersgate Street, as a residence for the Bishops of London. For this he paid £5200.[3] Peter

---

[1] These memorable words are now also inscribed in the church above the crypt.

[2] See Milman, *St. Paul's*, pp. 113, 114, note.

[3] Chalmers, *Biog. Dict.*, xxvii. 446.

Cunningham, F.S.A., in his *Handbook of London, Past and Present*,[1] says that the old

" London House, St. Paul's Churchyard, the inn or town-house of the Bishops of London, was pulled down and built into tenements about the year 1650 (see *A Discovery shewing the great Advantages of New Buildings*, 4to 1678, p. 11)."

But, earlier in the same work, Cunningham says—

" Aldersgate Street—nearly opposite Shaftesbury House stood *Peter House*, the town-house of Henry Pierrepont, Marquis of Dorchester, converted into a prison by Cromwell and his colleagues (*Dugdale's Troubles*, p. 568), and subsequently bought by the see of London, when the Great Fire had destroyed the episcopal residence in St. Paul's Churchyard."[2]

Bishop Henchman died in London House, Aldersgate Street, in 1675. Here, too, Dr. Compton, who succeeded Sheldon in the bishopric of London, lived. To his care King Charles II committed the care and education of his two nieces, the Princesses Mary and Anne, both of whom were confirmed and married by him—the

---

[1] Lond., 1850, p. 300.
[2] *Ibid.*, p. 6. " Henry Pierrepoint's house did not acquire the name of *London house* till after the destruction of the old palace near St. Paul's by the great fire."—Pennant, *Some Account of London*, 5th ed., p. 329.

former to William, Prince of Orange, the latter to George, Prince of Denmark. It was in Compton's tenure of London House that Princess Anne, later Queen, fled from Whitehall at the Revolution. John Milton also lived there. Philips, in his *Life of Milton*,[1] describes London House, Aldersgate Street, as

"a pretty garden-house, at the end of an entry, and therefore the fitter for his turn, by reason of the privacy, besides that there are few streets in London more free from noise."

London House in Aldersgate Street has long since been sold, and the present house of the Bishops of London in St. James' Square, rebuilt by Archbishop Howley when Bishop of London, substituted.

Reference must here be made to Sheldon's connection with the Library at Lambeth. Archbishop Bancroft, who died November 2, 1610, in his will, left all the books in his library at Lambeth to the archbishops, his successors in the primacy. To him is due the first collection of books which was to become a permanent possession of the See of Canterbury. It appears that a large portion of the Archbishop's books

[1] A·D., 1694, p. xx.

had formerly belonged to Robert Dudley, Earl of Leicester, the once powerful favourite of Queen Elizabeth.[1] This tradition is supported by the fact that the name and arms of Leicester are found in several of the volumes which formed part of Archbishop Bancroft's original gift. The books were left conditionally, inasmuch as the archbishop for the time being was to bind himself to leave them entire to his successor. They remained at Lambeth until the approach of the Great Rebellion, when, at Selden's suggestion, they were removed for safety to Cambridge.[2] After the Restoration, Archbishop Juxon demanded the restoration of the books, but, dying shortly after, Sheldon secured their being returned to Lambeth.

" The Great Cloisters of Lambeth palace were quadrangular in form, lying between the south side of the Chapel and the north end of the Hall, with the Guard-room on the east, and on the west opening out into the outer courtyard, and commanding a view of the Thames. Aubrey (*Antiquities of Surrey*, i. 9), who was his contemporary, ascribes the building of these Galleries over the Cloisters to Archbishop Sheldon : but Lysons (*Environs of London*, i. 265) suggests that he only restored them, and adapted them to

[1] See Aubrey, *Survey of Surrey*, v. 277.
[2] See Le Neve, 87.

the purposes of a Library, for the reception of Bancroft's legacy, which he succeeded in recovering from the University of Cambridge. This is far more probable, for Galleries undoubtedly existed here in Elizabeth's time." [1]

Writing in the year 1714, that is but thirty-seven years after Sheldon's death,[2] Walker, in his *Sufferings of the Clergy*,[3] expressly states that " He also erected the Fair Library at Lambeth-House": Anthony à Wood's statement [4] is to the same effect.

It is of interest to observe that Archbishop Potter (A.D. 1715–1737) was the first to style the manor-house of Lambeth " palace," and official documents are still dated *apud domum*, " at our house," at Lambeth. Archbishop Sheldon concludes his deed of gift of the Sheldonian Theatre, Oxford, in 1669—" Datis apud Ædes nostras Lambethanas," [5] and he dates a letter of 1665, " at my manor-house at Lambeth," and other letters of 1670 and 1672 from " Lambeth house."

---

[1] J. Cave-Browne, *Lambeth Palace* (Blackwood), Edin. and Lond., 1882, pp. 52, 53.
[2] Sheldon died November 9, 1677.
[3] Part II., p. 98.
[4] *Athen. Oxon.*, vol. ii. p. 1164.
[5] *Historia et Antiquitates Universitatis Oxonienses*, 1674, lib. ii., fol. 27.

"When Addington was bought, Lambeth had been for some years the only remaining residence of a prelate who, in the middle ages, had been able to travel from Harrow to Canterbury, and from Canterbury far into Sussex, without resting a night in any but his own houses."[1]

Henry Wharton (A.D. 1664-1695), in enumerating the sums which Sheldon bestowed on public purposes, adds, that he abated in his fines for the augmentation of vicarages the sum of £1680, and that he gave towards the repair of St. Paul's Cathedral, before the Great Fire of London in 1666, the sum of £2169, 17s. 10d., and for the repairs of his houses at Fulham, Lambeth, and Croydon the sum of £4500: to All Souls Chapel, Trinity College Chapel, Christchurch, Oxford, and to Lichfield Cathedral, £450. When Sheldon became Bishop of London, the leases having expired, he abated in his fines no less than £17,733, including apparently the sum of £1680 referred to above.[2]   Walker states that Sheldon

"bestowed great and large sums of money annuàlly, some to public, and some to private charities; and at his death £1500 more to

---

[1] Loftie, *Hist. of London*, 1883, vol. ii. p. 272.
[2] See Chalmers, *Biograph. Dict.*, xxvii. 446.

LADY CHAPEL OF OLD ST. PAUL'S CATHEDRAL

the same purposes. Insomuch, that it afterwards appeared by his book and accounts that he had lain out above £63,000 in uses of piety and charity."[1]

Sheldon was greatly interested in the Church beyond the seas.[2]

[1] Walker, *Sufferings of Clergy*, ii. 98.
[2] *Dict. Nat. Biog.*, *sub.* "Sheldon, Gilbert."

M

CHAPTER IX

SHELDON'S CHARACTER

Relation of conduct to character—Unfriendly attitude of the historians of Sheldon's time—His apparent severity against Nonconformists—The reasons thereof—The Puritan characteristics of the day—Sheldon held to be a politician rather than a divine—Comparative neglect by historians—Their unfair treatment of Sheldon—Opinion of him at All Souls, Oxford—His modesty concerning his gift of the Sheldonian Theatre—His generosity suffered to overshadow his administrative capacity—Some estimate of his munificence—Sheldon a patron of men of letters—The debt which literature owes to him never fully realised—His diligence and tact—His testimony to righteousness, and what it cost him—His courage—His portraits—Reference to Sheldon in Clarendon's will—His friends and associates—Sheldon's will—His epitaph—His tomb at Croydon—Ralph Sheldon and Dolben—Samuel Parker's testimony to Sheldon's character—Charles the First's affection for Sheldon—Clarendon's letter to Sheldon—Overton on Sheldon's character—Sheldon's detractors.

It remains to make some attempt to appreciate the character of the subject of this biography. The task is by no means easy. To describe the inner character of anyone whom we have not known personally, or with whom we have not been contemporaries, is ever difficult in the doing.

Moreover, "Who among men knoweth the things of a man, save the spirit of the man, which is in him?"[1] And, in the present instance, the attempt to read aright the personal characteristic traits of Gilbert Sheldon has its own peculiar difficulties.

Of his personal or private life we know next to nothing. All the records regarding him which have come down to us are concerned with him in the glare of public life, as Warden, Bishop, and Archbishop. Whilst it is a commonplace that conduct forms character, it is equally true to say that conduct reveals character; and it is by this latter truth that we must of necessity be guided in forming true and just ideas and opinions concerning that which he, Gilbert Sheldon, really was at his heart's core, in his inner being. It is, moreover, to our extreme disadvantage, that those of his day who wrote about him were his enemies, whose unfriendly attitude towards him blinded their eyes to his moral greatness, and perverted their judgment concerning him. To approach any subject in a hostile attitude of mind is fatal to fairness of estimate, for prejudice perverts a true judgment.

Personal wrongs done to Gilbert Sheldon,

---

[1] I Cor. ii. 11.

wrongs done, even unto death, to the monarch he loved and served, wrongs done to the Church of which he was so loyal a minister, had formed in him an attitude of apparent severity against the wrong-doers—against the Nonconformists as a class. And since these were the chief historians of the period, his name has been handed down blackened with all the obloquy which reciprocated dislike can overshadow a memory. It was his lot to be brought into close contact with the leading Puritans of the time. The hypocrisy of certain of the Puritan party bred in Sheldon's mind a profound contempt, and led him to suspect all pretence to special piety as a mere cloak for disloyalty, and even for dishonesty. Sheldon's special aversion from all forms of cant and unreality—an admirable trait in his character —is revealed in his advice to the "young noblemen and gentlemen," to which reference is made later in these pages—

"Let it be your principal care to become honest men, and afterwards be as devout and religious as you will: no piety will be of any advantage to yourselves or anyone else unless you are honest and moral men."

An impartial historian, in reference to the Puritans of Sheldon's day, has recorded that—

CHOIR OF MODERN ST. PAUL'S CATHEDRAL, LOOKING WEST

From an old engraving

"it was impossible to distinguish between the saint and the hypocrite, as soon as godliness became profitable: even amongst really earnest Puritans, prosperity disclosed a pride, a worldliness, a selfish hardness which had been hidden in the hour of persecution."[1]

The mutual dislike between Sheldon and the Puritans was doubtless accentuated and even embittered by the disputings and contentions of the conferences between the Bishops and the Nonconformists held at the Savoy, of which he was Master. The conferences accomplished nothing, and the episcopalians and the presbyterians parted in anger. The buffoonery which Sheldon encouraged in his hall at Lambeth, in holding up the Puritan mannerisms to ridicule, and which so greatly shocked Pepys, seems to show the exaggerated lengths to which his dislike of presbyterianism carried him. This regrettable incident certainly reveals his sense of humour.

That the circumstances of the time served to exhibit Gilbert Sheldon in the light of a politician and statesman, rather than as a divine and father in God, cannot be doubted: it could hardly have been otherwise. But it is scarcely open to doubt

---

[1] J. R. Green, *Short Hist. of the English People*, Lond., 1874, pp. 590, 591.

that few great men have been more successfully defrauded of their just claim to respect and admiration than Sheldon. From all we know of him and his great work for both Church and State, it is amazing to find so comparatively little said of him in our many historical accounts of his time. It has been the misfortune of few great man to have been so utterly deserted by modern writers, even of his own way of thinking. To make some attempt, however imperfect, to reinstate Gilbert Sheldon in his true position on the stage of history, is, to say the least, a mere act of common justice to a great memory. At the close of this chapter I venture to introduce the statements of the leading authors who, as it has been truly said, 'have successfully conspired to depose him from the place which he occupied in the view of the men of his own time.' Such a method may possibly disclose the way in which the history of the English Church has not infrequently suffered perversion, and, thus twisted out of recognition, has come down to our day unchallenged, and accepted without examination or question.

As to what was thought of Sheldon by his contemporaries at Oxford, we learn from the inscription at the foot of the fine plate of All

Souls College, engraved by David Loggan and published two years before Sheldon died, which compares him with the great Henry Chicheley, the Founder of the College and Archbishop of Canterbury in the early part of the fifteenth century—"Gilbertus Sheldon Archiep : Cantuar : et Sede Successor, et Divino Animo magni Chichley ἔκτυπος, inter bosce Parietes olim creuit." [1]

Of Sheldon's conspicuous moral courage, in withstanding Archbishop Laud, and in rebuking King Charles the Second, we have already spoken, as also of his being the first to protest against the common and popular profanity of identifying the Bishop of Rome with the " Anti-Christ." The man who could hold his own against William Laud in the height of his power in Church and State, and defy public opinion, had no small amount of moral courage and independence of character.

Sheldon appears to have been a man who set his face against ostentation, and who shunned public notoriety. Like his successor in the primacy, William Sancroft, Gilbert Sheldon had raised himself from obscurity to fame, by sheer force of his own merits and ability. The son

---

[1] *Oxonia Illustrata, delineavit et sculpsit Dav. Loggan,* Oxoniæ e Theatro Sheldoniano, A.D. MDCLLV.

of a domestic servant of Lord Shrewsbury's household, he had stepped out from a comparatively humble position to occupy the highest posts both in the University and the Church. And, in spite of this, we find him keeping in the background at the Savoy Conference, where we should naturally expect to see him to the fore. Witness also his refusal to be present at the opening of the Theatre which he so generously built at Oxford, or even to see it to the end of his days. It is not easy, in our own day, to imagine any donor of a public building on the vast scale of the Sheldonian Theatre, Oxford, and set apart for University functions, being absent on the occasion of laying the foundation stone and on that of the opening of such. And we can only attribute Sheldon's keeping away to his desire to shun observation and to avoid praise and thanks for his munificent gift. In providing this place of assembly, we have proof of his reverence for holy places and things and his desire to save St. Mary's, Oxford, from desecration. For, before the Theatre was built, the Encaenia, with its then accompanying ribaldry, had been held in the Church of St. Mary the Virgin, to Sheldon's evident distress. His dislike of ostentation is evidenced in his wish, expressed in

CHOIR OF MODERN ST. PAUL'S CATHEDRAL, LOOKING EAST

From an old plate

his will, to be buried "very privately"—a wish which was rightly respected, for "He was buried, the 16 Nov. 1677, at Croydon with little solemnity, for soe he desired."[1]

In Cary's *Memorials of the Civil War*[2] we find many indications of the assistance he rendered to such men as Bishop Wren and other distressed members of the loyalist party. From a letter signed "your most obliged and most affectionate friend and hearty servant, Jeremy Taylor," and dated "April 11, 1653," we learn that Sheldon had rendered pecuniary help to the man whose intrusion upon All Souls, Oxford, he had in conscience resisted—this intrusion by Laud had evidently been forgiven and forgotten. And this leads us to speak of the extraordinary liberality of Sheldon. It is as a man of great liberality that his name has been handed down to posterity. So great was this generosity that it has been allowed to overshadow his splendid administrative capacity and his moral excellence. At Oxford his munificence can never be forgotten. Having contributed £1000 towards building the Theatre which perpetuates his name, and no other benefactors coming forward, Sheldon took

[1] Ashmole MSS., Bodleian Lib., 860. 400.
[2] See vol. i. pp. 332–6.

upon himself the whole expense, which amounted to more than £20,000, and, in addition, he bequeathed a further sum of £2,000 for repairs and the establishment of a printing-house. We have scarcely any record of munificence on so large a scale, on behalf of charitable objects for the public good, as that which he showed throughout his long life. We have no means of knowing the amounts he spent in supporting the ruined clergy and educating candidates for the ministry during the Great Rebellion, and in relief of the two kings whom he so loyally and devotedly served; but it has been estimated that he gave about £66,000 to various charitable and public objects.[1] His treasurer, the person best fitted to know, estimated the amount at £72,000. In our own day this latter figure would represent some £350,000, if not more, of our money. In striking contrast with this royal generosity and princely munificence, is the desire expressed in Sheldon's will—

"My body I desire may be devoutly buried, but very privately and speedily, that my funerall may not wast much of what I leave behind me for better uses."

Unmarried, Sheldon lived for the common good.

[1] See Wood, *Athenæ Oxonienses*, vol. ii. p. 1164.

From Anthony à Wood's *Athenæ Oxonienses*
and other sources (alluded to previously in this
Life) we learn how generous and encouraging a
patron Sheldon was of men of letters. The debt
which literature owes to him has never yet been
fully realised or adequately acknowledged.

During the closing years of Dr. Juxon's life,
Gilbert Sheldon, Bishop of London, had been
virtually primate: on Juxon's death in 1663 he
became so in fact. In the exercise of this exalted
office Sheldon's splendid administrative capacity
has been universally acknowledged even by his
enemies, and they were many. By his diligence,
vigilance, admirable tact, and munificent generosity the wounds of the Church of England,
inflicted during the convulsions of the Commonwealth, were successfully tended and in great
measure healed. As was the case with his life-
long friend Clarendon, his powerful influence for
good upon Charles II, and his corrupt and profligate Court, gradually withered. The King, fast
sinking into the mire of disgusting debauchery,
resented Sheldon's interference with the gratifi-
cation of his shameless and unbridled lusts. We
know how he lost the royal favour for rebuking
the King for ·his abominable adultery—even
Burnet, Sheldon's great detractor, admits this—

for Swift tells us that the Archbishop on this account "had refused the Sacrament to the King for living in adultery."[1]   Charles the Second's treatment of Sheldon in this matter only serves to exemplify our Lord's teaching contained in the last of the eight Beatitudes, " Blessed are they that have been persecuted for righteousness sake " —a beatitude which describes the treatment which all who have His character must expect at the hands of those who are stung by its very beauty and are hardened by its very sanctity.   To his everlasting honour, Gilbert Sheldon bore his splendid testimony in a great and holy cause, regardless of consequences.   When we consider the whole situation, his courageous action in rebuking vice in high places compels our admiration.   Sheldon smoothed the path for Ken to follow in his steps, though the righteous protest of the latter prelate met with very different treatment at the hands of Charles II from that which he meted out to the former.

That Gilbert Sheldon was essentially a brave man is further evidenced by his conduct previously during the Plague of London.   Echard relates that Sheldon "firmly continued all the

---

[1] Note in Burnet's *Hist. of his own Time*, Univ. Press, 1832, vol. i. p. 464.

time of the greatest danger,"[1] staying at his
post at Lambeth, when everyone who could had
fled the stricken and doomed city. Would Gilbert
Burnet, Sheldon's great detractor, or any of his
opponents have acted with the same self-sacri-
ficing heroism in such a desperate situation? It
may be doubted.

The two portraits[2] of Sheldon hanging in
Lambeth Palace, and also the portraits of him at
All Souls College, Oxford, represent a somewhat
severe and almost forbidding expression of face,
and exhibit a self-reliant reserve, which goes
some way to account for his not having secured
the general esteem and due recognition of his
contemporaries beyond Oxford—for his failure
to attain to that position in the pages of the
history of the Church of England since the
Reformation for which his natural talents, steady
consistency, magnificent generosity, and conspicuous career justly entitled him.

One of the last glimpses we are allowed of
Sheldon is obtained through the will of Lord
Clarendon, which was dated from Rouen, De-

---

[1] *Hist. of England*, iii. 142.

[2] Of these two portraits one is copied from the picture of Sheldon
in Broom Hall, presented by Archbishop Cornwallis ; the other
is by an unknown artist, apparently a copy from one by David
Loggan, formerly in the possession of the Earl of Home. Of the
latter Vertue has published an admirable engraving.

cember 11, 1674. Of these two great men it has been said by a modern writer of distinction—

" The fastest of friendships, maintained in prosperity and adversity for half a century, in the classic society of Lord Falkland's open mansion, the martial excitement of the University fortress, the vicissitudes of exile, the guidance of two kings, the reorganisation of a shattered nation, the struggle with high-placed vice, the common loss of Court favour, the second exile, and the quiet preparation for death, finds its last expression in these directions to his sons." [1]

In his will, Clarendon, speaking of Sheldon, Archbishop of Canterbury, and Duppa, Bishop of Winchester, wrote : " I do entreat that they would be suitors to his Majesty on my children's behalf." [2]

The perusal of Dr. Sheldon's will, which Mr. Burrows printed for the first time [3] from the collection of MSS. in Codrington's Library, All Souls College, Oxford, gives further insight into the mind of the subject of this biography. It runs as follows :—

" I, Gilbert Sheldon, Archbishop of Canterbury, being in good health of body and sound and perfect

---

[1] Burrows, *Worthies of All Souls*, p. 249.
[2] *Clarendon State Papers*, iii. 736.
[3] *Worthies of All Souls*, p. 250.

in memory and understanding (God be praised for it) doe make and ordaine this my last Will and Testament in manner and forme following. First, I recommend my soule into the mercifull hands of my gracious Redeemer, my only Lord, Saviour and Master Jesus Christ, relying wholly upon his goodness and mercy for my salvation, giving him most humble thanks for calling mee by his Gospel and grace to his knowledge and obedience, abhorring all sects, sidings and tyranny in religion, holding fast the true orthodox profession of the Catholique faith of Christ, foretold by the prophets and preached to the world by Christ himself, his blessed Apostles and their successors, being a true member of his Catholique Church within the Communion of a living part thereof, the present Church of England, desiring God to confirme mee in this ffaith and in all Christian charity and his holy feare to my lives end. My body I desire may be devoutly buried, but very privately and speedily, that my funerall may not wast much of what I leave behind me for better uses."

The epitaph of Sheldon contains the following lines :—

Omnibus negotiis par, Omnibus titulis superior, in rebus adversis magnus, in prosperis bonus, utriusque fortunæ Dominus, pauperum parens, literatorum patronus, ecclesiæ stator : De tanto viro pauca dicere non expedit, multa non opus :

nôrunt præsentes, posteri vix credent: Octogenarius animam piam et coelo maturam Deo reddidit V. Id. ix^{bris} 1677.[1]

Writing in his *Diary*, July 13, 1700, less than three years after Sheldon's death, John Evelyn says :—

"The tombs in the church at Croydon of Archbishops Grindal, Whitgift, and other Archbishops, are fine and venerable ; but none comparable to that of the late Archbishop Sheldon, which, being all of white marble, and of a stately ordinance and carvings, far surpassed the rest, and I judge would cost not less than £700 or £800."[2]

There is a print of this monument in Lysons' *Environs of London*, art. "Croydon," vol. i. p. 193. The sculptured recumbent figure is excellent in workmanship, but wretched in design. This monument was erected in the Archbishop's memory by his heir, Sir Joseph Sheldon, then

---

[1] "Equal to every business, superior to every title of honour, great in adversity, good in prosperity, master of either fortune, the father of the poor, the patron of men of letters, a pillar of the Church : concerning so great a man it is inexpedient to say little, it is needless to say much : those now living know, those to come will hardly believe. In his eightieth year he yielded up to God his holy soul, ready for heaven. November 9, 1677." For transcription of epitaph in full, see Appendix v.

[2] *Diary and Correspondence of John Evelyn*, ed. Bray, London, 150, vol. ii. p. 361.

SHELDON'S TOMB, CROYDON CHURCH

lately Lord Mayor of London, son of his elder brother, Ralph Sheldon,[1] of Stanton, Staffordshire. A photograph of the Archbishop's tomb has been taken specially for this work, and is reproduced amongst the illustrations.

As to how the character and conduct of Gilbert Sheldon in his later days struck competent witnesses, there is but one of his contemporaries who writes as an observer, namely, Samuel Parker, Bishop of Oxford in the time of James II. Parker was an able man, who as Sheldon's domestic chaplain had good opportunities of judging in this matter. In his *Commentarii de rebus sui temporis*, a posthumous work, Parker writes—

"Archbishop Sheldon was a man of undoubted piety, but though he was very assiduous at

---

[1] Ralph Sheldon, described by Walker in his *Sufferings of the Clergy* (Part ii. p. 107, sub. 'John Dolben'), as "elder brother to the suffering Warden of All Souls College,' married his daughter to the Rev. John Dolben, who thus became Gilbert Sheldon's nephew by marriage. After the Restoration, John Dolben became Canon of Christchurch, and "by the favour of Dr. Sheldon, his wife's uncle, successively, Archdeacon of London, Clerk of the Closet, Dean of Westminster, Bishop of Rochester, Lord Almoner, and in 1683 was translated to the Archiepiscopal See of York" (Walker, *Ibid.*). Dolben, with others, kept up the devotions of the Church of England and ministered the Sacraments to the suffering Royalists who remained in Oxford during the Commonwealth in a house opposite Merton College (*Ibid.*). Evelyn says in his *Diary*, August 25, 1678—"After evening prayer, visited Mr. Sheldon, (nephew of the late Archbishop of Canterbury) and his pretty melancholy garden"; he would be son of Ralph Sheldon.

N

prayers, yet he did not set so great a value on them as others did, nor regarded so much worship as the use of worship, placing the chief point of religion in the practice of a good life. In his daily discourse he cautioned those about him not to deceive themselves with an half religion, nor to think that Divine Worship was confined within the walls of the church, the principal part of it being without doors, and consisting in being conversant with mankind. If men led an upright, sober, chaste life, then and not till then, they might look upon themselves as religious; otherwise it would signify nothing what form of religion bad men followed, or to what Church they belonged. Then having spoken to this effect he added with a kind of exultation and joy:—'Do well and rejoice.'

"His advice to young noblemen and gentlemen, who by their parents' commands resorted daily to him, was always this: 'Let it be your principal care to become honest men, and afterwards be as devout and religious as you will. No piety will be of any advantage to yourselves or anybody else, unless you are honest moral men.' He had a great aversion to all pretences of extraordinary piety which covered real dishonesty; but had a sincere affection for those whose religion was attended with integrity of manners. His worthy notions of religion meeting with an excellent temper in him gave him that even tranquillity of mind by which he was ever himself and always the same in adversity and prosperity, neither overvalued nor despised life, nor feared nor wished for death; but lived agreeably to himself and others."

Surely these words describe a moral character which is entirely admirable and worthy of imitation in every age. For, according to the teaching of Jesus Christ conveyed in the Sermon on the Mount,[1] it is not mere barren orthodoxy, or the observance of the outward forms of religion, which is the essential thing, but rather a holy life. In that great discourse He does not require of us to do such and such actions, but rather to endeavour to be in character such and such kind of persons. If there was any form of vice against which Jesus Christ set His face more than another, it was hypocrisy and formalism, the punctilious performance of the external acts of religion apart from inner morality and unconstrained by corresponding righteousness of living. And what Gilbert Sheldon had by sad experience learnt in the times when Puritanism was in the ascendancy was to hate cant and unreality. That King Charles the Martyr should have had an affectionate regard for Sheldon, as we learn from Samuel Parker was the case, is quite consistent with all we know

[1] See particularly, St. Matt. vii. 21 ff.

about this great and good man. Of Lord Clarendon's regard for Sheldon, we have already spoken; but it may not be amiss to reproduce a passage from a letter from Clarendon to Sheldon, as an illustration of that regard. It is amongst the Sheldon papers in the Bodleian Library, Oxford.

I beg your grace a thousand pardons for the presumption in intruding in an affair of this nature, (his lordship had objected to the translation of the bishop of Limerick to an English bishopric,) which, God knows, nothing could have led me into but my faithful and filial duty to the Church, whose peace and lustre I pray for as much as I do for myself. Forgive me, and give me your benediction.

Overton, who describes Archbishop Sheldon as "that arch-enemy of nonconformity," gives his judgment impartially concerning him—

"Among the Caroline divines the most influential was, beyond all question, Gilbert Sheldon. He was made Bishop of London; but, owing to the age and infirmities of Juxon, he was virtually primate from the moment of the King's return, and became actually so on that good old man's death. Taking the prominent part he did in politico-ecclesiastical matters, there is no wonder that his character should have been differently described according to the different views of the describers. The discrepancies between the various estimates of him are almost ludicrous. But after all, it is not very difficult to reconcile them. On certain points all are agreed. His munificence was unbounded. . . . He was a man of undaunted courage; he stayed manfully at his post at Lambeth all through the Plague; he did not shrink from rebuking his royal master, thereby forfeiting the King's favour, which he never regained. He was a most generous patron of learning; if the prelates of the Restoration period shed a lustre on the Church, as they surely did, Sheldon must be credited with much the largest share in their appointment. 'Archbishop Sheldon had the keys of the Church for a great time in his power; and could admit into it and keep out of it whom he pleased' (Dr. Pope's *Life of Bishop Seth Ward*, 1697, p. 53). He had obviously the gift of attaching his friends most devotedly to him. He was emphatically a strong man, with a firm will of his own, perfectly straightforward and candid, without a particle of cant. A man of whom all this can be said has strong claims upon our regard. But, on the other hand, we can gather, even from his panegyrists' accounts and from his own recorded acts and words, that he was more of a statesman than a divine, that spiritual-mindedness was, to say the least, not a conspicuous trait in his character, that he took a leading part in the persecution of nonconformists, and that his disgust at hypocrisy led him, like many others, into the anti-puritanical reaction of the time, far too much in the opposite direction." [1]

And, be it noted, that though the sworn foe of nonconformity and Puritanism, Sheldon presented the living of Ashwell to Ralph Cudworth, the close associate of Cromwell all through the Commonwealth, and that he "often treated very kindly" Thomas White, the ejected lecturer of St. Bride's, whom he "protected at the chappel at Ludgate." [2] Such actions as these serve to exhibit a fine generosity of character in one who, when principle was at stake, set his face like a flint.

We would fain bring our sketch of the character and life of Gilbert Sheldon to a conclusion at this point, but it is needful to refer, as a matter of justice to his memory, to certain gross misrepresentations for which the historians Neal and Burnet are chiefly responsible. The latter says,

" Sheldon was esteemed a learned man before the wars : but he was now engaged so deep in politicks, that scarce any prints of what he had

---

[1] Overton, *Life in the English Church*, 1885, pp. 19, 20.
[2] Calamy, *Account of Ejected Ministers*, ii. 31.

been remained. He was a very dextrous man in
business, had a great quickness of apprehension,
and a very true judgment. He was a generous
and charitable man. He had a great pleasant-
ness of conversation, perhaps too great. He had
an art, that was peculiar to him, of treating all
that came to him in a most obliging manner : but
few depended much on his professions of friend-
ship. He seemed not to have a deep sense of
religion, if any at all :[1] and he spoke of it most
commonly as of an engine of government,
and a matter of policy. By this means the
King came to look on him as a wise and honest
clergyman."[2]

This passage appeared thus far in the early
editions of Burnet's History, before Dr. Routh
published his Oxford edition, in which certain
passages, suppressed by earlier editors, were
restored in brackets. One of these cautiously
omitted passages follows immediately the quota-
tion given above—"though he had less virtue and
less religion." So outrageous and malicious was
this libel on Sheldon's character, that the earlier
editors refused to insert it in their editions of
Burnet's posthumous work. Suppression of facts

---

[1] N. Salmon (*Lives of English Bishops*, 1733) describes this
statement of Burnet as 'unwarrantable.'

[2] Burnet, *Hist. of his own Time*, Lond., 1766, vol. i. p. 247.

is always a mistake, and particularly in this instance; for the suppressed sentence drags into light what we should have readily suspected without it—namely, that Burnet's information was derived from untrustworthy and hostile sources. In fact it displays a degree of positive *animus* against Sheldon. To say the least, we should have imagined that Burnet's actual knowledge of a man whose life and actions must have been fairly well known to him, as a contemporary, would have saved him from attributing "little virtue and less religion" to Gilbert Sheldon, the intimate friend and close associate of such good and honourable men as Clarendon, Falkland, Laud, Jeremy Taylor, Sanderson, Hammond, and Morley, the spiritual adviser of King Charles the Martyr, and the courageous rebuker of his degenerate son, Charles II.

Nevertheless this account of Sheldon, from the pen of Burnet, in its suppressed form, has been adopted without any carefulness of enquiry as to its veracity by most writers of English history! And this is not all; the Puritan historian, Daniel Neal, has had the temerity to add to Burnet's libel, by stating, without the least pretence of authority or evidence—"He made a jest of religion any further than it was a political engine

of State."[1] The unworthy device of blackening
an opponent's memory has rarely been carried
to a higher pitch of perfection. Another arrow
dipped in the same poison is aimed at Gilbert
Sheldon by Henry Hallam; evidently following
verbally Daniel Neal, whom he describes as "a
controversialist, prejudiced, and loving the interests of his own faction better than truth,[2] and
not very scrupulous about misrepresenting an
adversary"—Hallam says, "Sheldon . . . is represented as a man who considered religion
chiefly as an engine of policy."[3] Hallam's blind
following of Burnet and Neal, his contemptuous
reference to the prophecy of that eminent historian, Lord Clarendon, regarding Sheldon's future
occupancy of the primacy, alluded to above[4]—
"it is said on somebody's authority that Sheldon
was born and bred to be Archbishop of Canterbury"[5]—are quite sufficient to damn him as an
unreliable detractor from the character and merits
of the great and eminent Gilbert Sheldon. Following the same unworthy lead, S. T. Coleridge
makes use of the outrageous words — "This
Sheldon, the most virulent enemy and poisoner

[1] Neal, *Hist. of the Puritans*, vol. ii. p. 708.
[2] *Constitutional Hist. of England*, Lond., 1829, vol. i. p. 279 *n*.
[3] *Ibid.*, vol. ii. p. 475.   [4] See p. 67.
[5] *Constitutional Hist. of England*, vol. ii. p. 525 *n*.

of the English Church." [1]   The reader may be left to form his or her own opinion as to the veracity and justice of all such unfavourable estimates of the character of Gilbert Sheldon, in the light of the leading outlines of his life as depicted in the foregoing pages.   As to the final result of such a comparison the present writer has no apprehensions whatever.   Sheldon's life speaks for itself, and it needs no apology.

It is painful to have to sound this jarring note in concluding our survey of the career of Sheldon, but it has seemed to the biographer a necessity. He believes that no one can study that eventful career without partiality or prejudice, as he has endeavoured to do, and not arrive at the well-founded conclusion, that Gilbert Sheldon was a man whose name and memory ought and deserves to be had in lasting reverence and honour.

[1] *Notes on English Divines*, ii. 22.

APPENDICES

APPENDIX I

ACCOUNT OF GILBERT SHELDON

Transcribed from *Athenæ Oxonienses* by Anthony à Wood, M.A. Second Edition, Lond., 1721, vol. ii., foll. 1162–1164.

GILBERT SHELDON, the youngest son of Rog. Sheldon of Stanton in Staffordshire, near to Ashbourne in Derbyshire, was born there on the 19th of July[1] 1598, and had his Christian name given to him at his Baptization by Gilbert, Earl of Shrewsbury, to whom his father was a menial servant. In the latter end of 1613 he became a Com. of Trin. Coll., and proceeding in Arts seven years after, was, in the year 1622, elected Fellow of that of Alls. and about the same time took holy Orders. Afterwards he was made domestic Chapl. to Tho. Lord Coventry, L. Keeper of the Great Seal, who finding him to be a man of parts, recommended him to K. Ch. I. as a person well versed in politics. In 1634 he proceeded in Divinity, being then, as it seems, Preb. of Gloc. in the latter end of the year following he was elected Warden of his Coll. About the same time he became Chapl. in Ord. to his Màj.

[1] This is a mistake for "June," as he was baptized on June 26.

was afterwards Clerk of his Closet, and by him designed to be Master of the Hospital called the Savoy, and Dean of Westm. that he might the better attend on his Royal Person; but the change of the times and Rebellion that followed, hindred his settlement in them. During the time of the said Rebellion he adhered to his Maj. and his cause, and therefore was not only ejected his Wardenship, but also imprisoned with Dr. H. Hammond in Oxon, and elsewhere, by the Visitors appointed by Parl. *an.* 1648, to the end that their eminency in the Univ. might not hinder their proceedings, and to keep them both from attending the K. at the Treaty in the Isle of Wight. After he was released, he retired to his friends in Staffordshire, Nottinghamshire, and Derbyshire, whence and where, from his own purse and from others which he made use of, he sent constantly moneys to the exiled King, followed his studies and devotions till matters tended to a happy restoration of his Maj. On the 4th of March 1659, Dr. Joh. Palmer, who had usurped his Wardenship almost 12 years, died, at which time there being an eminent foresight of his Maj. return, there was no election made of a successor, only a restitution of Dr. Sheldon; who instead of re-taking possession in person (which he never did) was made Dean of his Maj. Chap. Royal, and nominated to succeed Dr. Juxon in London, upon his translation thence to Canterbury: whereupon being consecrated

thereunto in the Chap. of K. Hen. VII. at Westm.
by the Bp. of Winchester (delegated thereunto
by Canterbury) assisted by York, Ely, Rochester
and Chichester, on the 28th of Oct. (S. Sim. and
Jude) *an.* 1660, sate there, as one thought fittest
to take charge and care of that great and popu-
lous City, till the decease of the said Dr. Juxon ;
and then being elected to succeed him in Canterbury by the Dean and Chapter thereof, on the
11th of Aug. 1663, the election was confirmed on
the 15th of the same month by his Majesty (to
whom Dr. Sheldon had been for some time
before one of his Privy Council) and thereupon
was translated with great solemnity in the Archb.
Chappel at Lambeth, the 31st of the said month.
. . . In 1667 Dr. Sheldon was elected Chancellor
of the Univ. of Ox. but was never installed, nor
ever was there after that time, no not so much as
to see his noble work called the Theatre, or ever
at Canterbury to be there personally installed
Archbishop, or upon any other occasion while he
was Archbishop. At length arriving at a fair
age, he surrendered up his soul to God on
Friday about seven of the clock at night, of the
9th of Nov. in sixteen hundred and seventy
seven : whereupon his body was privately in-
terred in the parochial church of Croyden in
Surrey, near to the tomb of Archb. Whitgift (according to his own special direction) upon Friday
evening, the 16th of the said month. Soon after
was a most stately monument erected over his

grave by his heir, Sir Joseph Sheldon, then lately
L. Mayor of London, son of his elder brother,
Ralph Sheldon of Stanton before mentioned,
with a large inscription thereon [here follows part
of the Latin inscription, quoted in full previously
in this volume]. He hath only extant *A Sermon
before the King at* Whitehall, *the* 28*th of* June
1660, *being the day of the solemn Thanksgiving
for the happy return of his Majesty*, on *Psal.* 18.
49 *Lond.* 1660. His works of piety and charity
were many in his lifetime, as (1) the building of
the Theatre at Oxon, which cost him more than
16 thousand pounds, besides his gift of £2,000 to
buy lands, worth an £100 *per an.* to keep it in
repair. This noble structure was built chiefly for
the celebration of the public *Acts*, yet since
neglected. (2) The fair Library at Lambeth
House, built at his own charge. (3) Two thousand pounds towards the structure of S. Paul's
Cathedral. (4) Considerable sums of money to
Trin. Coll. in Oxon, and Trin. Coll. in Camb.
besides great and large sums of money annually
bestowed, some to public, and some to private
charities. His legacies at his death for charitable
uses came to £1,500 which afterwards were paid,
part to Alls. Coll., part to the church of Canterbury, part to the Hospital of Harbledown in
Kent, and the rest to indigent persons. I have
heard Sir Joseph Sheldon before-mentioned say
(who dying the 16th of Aug. 1681, was buried
near to the body of his uncle) that from the time

CLOISTERS OF LAMBETH PALACE LIBRARY

From an old engraving

of Dr. Sheldon's being made Bishop of London, to the time of his death, it did appear in the book of his accounts, that he had bestowed upon public, pious and charitable uses, about three-score and six thousand pounds.

APPENDIX II

Account of Gilbert Sheldon's Ejection from the Wardenship of All Souls College, Oxford, A.D. 1648; reprinted from Walker's "Attempt towards recovering an Account of the Numbers and Sufferings of the Clergy of the Church of England, etc., in the late Times of the Grand Rebellion." Lond. 1714; Part II. p. 98.

ALL SOULS COLLEGE, OXFORD.

GILBERT SHELDON, D.D., *Wardenship*, ETC.

" He was born at Stanton in Staffordshire, and elected Fellow of this College from that of Trinity in this University [Wood, *Ath.*, vol. ii. p. 678]. Afterwards he became Chaplain to the Lord Keeper Coventry, Prebendary of Gloucester, and about the end of 1635 was advanced to the Wardenship. [May 2, 1633, he was also admitted to the Vicarage of Hackney in Middlesex.—Newc., *Rep. Eccles.*, vol. i. p. 620.] About the same time also he became Chaplain to his Majesty, and was by him designed for the Mastership of the Savoy, and the Deanery of

Westminster, had not the Rebellion prevented it. During which he adhered stedfastly to the royal cause; and when the Oxford Visitation came on, strenuously opposed it. March 27, 1648, he honestly and boldly told the Visitors, 'That he could not with a safe conscience submit to them'; for which, three days after, they deprived him of his Wardenship, and substituted in his room one John Palmer [Wood, *Ant.*, L. i. p. 397], a Bachelor of Physic; though it was directly contrary to the statutes of the College. April 3 following, the paper for his expulsion was affixed to his lodgings, and ⋅at the same time Palmer's election was published. The 13th of that month also, the Visitors (and the Earl of Pembroke at the head of them) came themselves to All Souls College in order to dispossess Dr. Sheldon by force, and put their new Warden in possession. At which time the Doctor pleaded on behalf of himself, that their commission did not reach him, because it bore date March 6, and authorised them to dispossess those only whom the Pàrliament or Committee had voted out before. Now the vote for his expulsion was not passed till March 30, which was three weeks after the date of their commission. This cost the Visitors an hour's debate; but at last Prynn, who was one of them, and at that time present, instead of untying, cut the knot in this manner: 'Although,' saith he, 'the Doctor is not within the letter, yet he is within the equity of the Commission, and the Parliament must not be fooled with.' And accordingly upon the resolution of this casuist, they proceed to deprive him of his freehold, strike his name out of the Buttery-book, substitute Palmer's in the place of it, and withal, order the Doctor into custody; for which the Earl of Pembroke alledged this reason—that he had not opened the Great Gate to him when he came thither. After this they broke open the lodging-doors, put Palmer in possession, and then hurried away the Doctor to prison; who, as he passed the streets, had a thousand prayers and blessings from the people [Wood, *Ant.*, L. i. p. 403].

"In this durance he continued above six months, and then the Reforming Committee set him at liberty (October 24, 1648) on condition, that he should immediately depart five miles from Oxon; that he should not go to the King in the Isle of Wight; and that he should give security to appear before them at four days' warning whenever cited [Wood, *Ant.*, L. i. p. 413]: After which he retired to his friends in Staffordshire, and the adjoining counties; from whence he constantly sent money (partly of his own, and partly what he collected from others) to his Majesty then in exile; and followed his studies and devotions, till matters tended to an happy Restoration.

"In 1659, Palmer the intruder died, and there being at that time a plain prospect of the Restoration, Dr. Sheldon was restored to his Wardenship, though he never appeared in person to repossess himself. Not long after, his Majesty became actually possessed of his throne, and then Dr. Sheldon was made Dean of the Chapel Royal, and soon after it succeeded Dr. Juxon in the See of London, as he did afterwards also in the archiepiscopal chair of Canterbury in 1663. He was also elected Chancellor of this University (Oxon) in the year 1667, and died November 9, 1677.

" It would be needless to tell the reader that the noble Theatre in Oxford was erected at his sole charge, which was that of £18,000. He also erected the fair Library at Lambeth house, gave £2,000 to St. Paul's Cathedral, considerable sums to Trinity Colleges in Oxford and Cambridge; bestowed great and large sums of money annually, some to public and some to private charities; and at his death gave £1,500 more to the same purposes: insomuch, that it afterwards appeared by his books and accounts, that he had lain out above £63,000 in uses of piety and charity.

" He hath nothing extant but a sermon before his Majesty at Whitehall, preached June 28, 1660, being the Solemn Day of Thanksgiving for the happy Restoration."

APPENDIX III

BAPTISMS—*Anno Dñi* 1648

Joane the daughter of Robert Sadler and his wife
was baptized May the 7th.

Thomas the sonne of William Smith and Anne
his wife was baptized June the 11th.

William the sonne of Matthew Turner and his
wife was baptized July the 5th.

Hannah the daughter of Thomas John Ju: and
Anne his wife was baptized Novem: the
second.

Joane the daughter of Thomas Titte and Dennis
his wife was baptized Decem: the 31th.

Williā the sonne of Tho: Juss Juni: and Mary
his wife was baptized ffeb: the 11th.

Edwarde the sonne of Edwarde Hobbie and
Elizabeth his wife was baptized ffeb: the
14th.

Mary the daughter of Edmund Kirwood &
Margaret his wife was baptized March the
17th.

MARRIAGES—*Anno Domini* 1648

No entries.

BURIALS—*Anno Domini* 1648

No entries.

BAPTISMS—*Anno Dñi* 1649

Anne the daughter of Thomas Edwards and his wife was baptized Aprill the 29th.

George the sonne of George Ckere and Joane his wife was baptized May the 31th.

John the sonne of John Symons and Ellen his wife was baptized July the first.

Joan the daughter of Gregory Juss and Rachel his wife was baptized Novem: the 15th.

Josias the sonne of Edmund Juss and his wife was baptized Febru: the 17th 1649.

Elizabeth the daughter of Edwarde Hobbie and Elizabeth his wife was baptized Mar: the 24th.

MARRIAGES—*Anno Domini* 1649

No entries.

BURIALS—*Anno Domini* 1649

No entries.

BAPTISMS—*Anno Dñi* 1650

Richard the sonne of Tho: Coles Juni and Anne
his wife was baptized June the 3d.

Thomas the sonne of Robert Sadler and his wife
was baptized July the 15th.

William the sonne of William Smith & Anne his
wife was baptized Aug: the 26th.

Mary the daughter of Williā Tyrrell and Elizabeth his wife was baptized Decem: the
26th.

Williā the sonne of John Coles & his wife was
baptized Decem: the 27th.

MARRIAGES—*Anno Domini* 1650

No entries.

BURIALS—*Anno Dñi* 1650

Mary the wife of Williā Tipping was buried
Aprill the 6th.

Edmund Kirwood was buried Aprill the 15th.

Annie the daughter of Willm and Elonor Coles
was buried the 26 of februarie.

COMMUNION-PLATE, ICKFORD CHURCH

The gift of Sheldon

APPENDIX **IV**

DAVID'S DELIVERANCE AND THANKSGIVING

A sermon preached before the King at Whitehall upon June 28, 1660, *being the day of Solemn Thanksgiving for the happy return of His Majesty.* By GILBERT SHELDON, D.D., and Dean of His Majesties Chappell Royall. Published by His Majesties Speciall Command.

PSALM 18. 49.

Therefore will I give thanks unto thee (O Lord) among the heathen, and sing praises unto thy Name.

The words before run thus.—Verse 46. *The Lord liveth, and blessed be my rock, and let the God of my salvation be exalted.* 47. *It is God that avengeth me, and subdueth the people under me.* 48. *He delivereth me from mine enemies, yea thou liftest me up above those that rise up against me ; thou hast delivered me from the violent man.* 49. *Therefore, &c.*

WHAT the argument of this Psalm is ; why, when, and by whom written, the Title shews, and tels us, that 'twas *David's*, made *in the day that the Lord delivered him from all his enemies, and from the hand of Saul.*

'Tis recorded (2 *Sam.* 22) after the Rebellion of *Absalom* and *Sheba*, and 'tis thought by some to be one of the best, if not the very best, that ever he made. I shall not meddle at all with the *mystical* or *Prophetical* sense of it, either as it relates to Christ or his Church, matters more proper for other times; but onely with the *Historical* or *Literal*, as it concerned *David*, and by his example all that succeed him in the like Dangers and Deliverances; even us at present, and proper and fit it is for us. For 'tis a *Psalm of Thanksgiving* throughout, and the Verses read unto you are a sum of the whole, a recapitulation of all that went before, where after a *Commemoration* of God's several *Deliverances*, he infers his own Duty, and so by consequence ours, in the words of the Text: Because thou hast so graciously, so mercifully delivered me from so many and great dangers,

Therefore will I give thanks unto thee (*O Lord*) *among the Heathen, and sing praises unto thy Name.*

Wherein be pleased to take notice with me of these three particulars.

1. Of *David delivered.*
2. Of *God his Deliverer.*
3. Of *David's thankfulnesse for his deliverance.*

Of these in order; and first, of the person delivered.

1. *David*, a *King*, and *Saint*, both which
intitle him to an especial interest in God's
good Providence: *Kings* are his *Deputies*,
Saints his *Friends;* and *David* no ordinary
King or *Saint*, but eminent in both relations;
an excellent Person, and gracious *King*, one
after God's own heart (*Acts* 13. 22), a Type
of *Christ;* and no marvel if such be delivered by him, if God have an especial care of
him. The *wonder* is, how so good a Man, so
gracious a Prince, should have Enemies and
Rebels, should fall into such dangers and afflictions, should need so many deliverances.

But if we consider it well, it's no wonder
neither; never was, never will be: For if we
look to the eminentest persons in all Ages of
the World, from the first man to this day, we
shall find that the best of Men and most godly,
have ever had many afflictions, many enemies,
and many the more for being so. The *Prophet*
complains 'twas his case, and that he suffered
much *because he followed the thing that good was*
(*Psal.* 38. 20). And St. *Paul* assures us, that *All*
(all without exception) *that will live godly in
Christ Jesus shall suffer persecution* (2 Tim. 3. 12),
and if there were no other cause, even for
their *godlinesse:* their Vertues are a reproach to
the wicked world, and cannot well be endured.

But reason enough for it there is besides; for
even in the *best*, there is something *amisse;* no
corn without chaff, nor gold without some dross:

All Saints are sinners, and sin will be punished in
God's children soonest of all, he least endures it
in them (*Psal.* 17. 14). 'Tis the wicked usually
that have *their portion in this life*, and that come
in no trouble like other men (*Psal.* 73. 5).
Prosperity in sin is their curse, a sad sign of
utter destruction, and the very next step to Hell
fire: But they who are designed for Heaven,
must pass thither *through much tribulation* (*Acts*
14. 22). There is ever an *Aegypt* in their way
to *Canaan.* Only this is their comfort, that
being under his *Rod*, they are not out of his
Care: Afflictions are their Physick; and by
them, *like Gold in the Furnace* (*Prov.* 27. 21),
they gain lustre, and lose no weight, are mended
here that they may be saved hereafter. No
marvel then if a *Saint* fall into trouble, if he need
deliverance; especially if a *King*, if a *Saint-
Royal.*

For no state or condition of men in the world
is so obnoxious to dangers as theirs: For man
by nature is proud and querulous, impatient of
government, greedy of liberty, ever restless and
pressing after new desires, always displeased with
the present, and thirsting after change; scarce
any content with their condition. Some are
ambitious and would be greater; others *covetous*
and would be richer; have suffered a repulse in
some unreasonable suits, have been restrained in
some exorbitant desires; injuries not to be forgiven
or forgotten. Some are *necessitous*, and so greedy;

some *revengeful,* and will be quarrelling; some *envious,* some *turbulent,* and delight in mischief, and many the like. Now all this crowd and throng of inordinate passions and humors dischargeth it self upon those in *power* and *place,* and hope to find ease by some publick disturbance, which they endeavour by all arts and wayes imaginable, that so in troubled waters they may catch that which quieter times would have derived upon persons of better merit.

And the condition of *Kings* gives some advantage to such designs; for they stand high, and all eyes are upon them, nothing they say or do escapes observation and censure; if any thing be amiss (as in the distraction of many cares, and multiplicity of much business, 'tis impossible but that some slips should happen, some errors be committed) they are sure to hear of them to their greatest disadvantage: a *Mote* will be called a *Beam,* a *Gnat* a *Camel;* and few will be multiplied into many.

'Twere happy with the world, were every man as *wise* as he thinks himself; but the *opinion of Wisdome* is the greatest part of *Folly,* and that the common disease of Mankind: and so much the worse, because they ever think themselves wisest in other men's business, are ever complaining they do not do their duty, especially *Governours,* whose great misfortune it is, that if all be well with us by their care and wisdom, we thank our selves for it; if any thing amiss, we blame them;

and what fals upon us by our own *sins*, we usually with great injustice impute to their *errors*. And which is still worse, if they cannot be justly charged with any miscarriage, yet that helps not: Innocency is no protection for them; their place and power is crime enough to pull them down, others would be where they are, who like the Devil (as St. *Bernard*) *Malunt miserè præesse, quam feliciter subesse;* had rather be miserable in power, than happy in subjection; and then to make way for their ambition, faults must be found, though there be none; and 'tis strange how far impudent *calumnies* prevail with a discontented people, and gain belief beyond all imagination, ever against sense and reason.

And therefore if you look upon the best of PRINCES in prophane stories, you shall find them by these Arts and wayes exercised as much as any, if not more; by *Mutinies, Seditions, Rebellions:* I forbear instances very obvious, and shall onely touch upon some we find registred in Scripture. And first upon *David* in the Text.

A vertuous and pious man, a great Souldier, a gracious Prince, one that wanted nothing to oblige a people to obedience and respect, *a man after God's own heart* (1 *Sam.* 13. 14), proposed as a pattern to *Solomon*, with a promise to entail his Kingdome and blessing upon him and his posterity, if he would *but walk in his steps* (2 *Chron.* 7. 17, 18), the measure and standard by which the succeeding Princes were

est of
s most
ed in
ions.

judged, *His heart was not perfect, as my servant David's ;* so of many : Or, *he did according to all that my servant David did ;* so of others, and that was thought commendations enough. His Vertues out-lived himself, and many generations fared the better for him ; *Solomon* the Father, and *Rehoboam* the Son, and many more preserved from utter ruine for his sake. And in the days of *Hezekiah* (above Three hundred years after) *Jerusalem* her selfe in greatest distress, defended by God, for his *own sake, and for his servant David's sake* (2 *Kings* 19. 34).

Yet this rare and excellent person, this gracious Prince, the very *light of Israel*, as his Subjects stiled him (2 *Sam.* 21. 17), was restless all his days ; I cannot reckon his *troubles*, because he himself says they were *innumerable* (*Psal.* 40. 12), nor his enemies that *hated him without cause*, and sought to *destroy him wrongfully*, for *they were mighty* (*Psal.* 38. 19), and *more than the hairs of his head* (*Psal.* 69. 4), and that of all sorts, from the gravest that *sate in the gates*, (the place of Judicature) vers. 12 down to the *Drunkards* and very scum of the people, the one *made songs*, the other put scorns *upon him* (*Psal.* 35. 15), slandered his *Person*, traduced his Government, which God himself never found fault with ; and at last took Arms against him, drove him from his *House* and *Imperial City*, forced him to flee he knew not whither, glad to take any way for present safety : And to make up his sorrows to the full, who should head these Rebels but his dearly beloved *Absalom!* who drew into conspiracy with him, besides the most of his Subjects, even his own *familiar friend whom he trusted, which did also eat of his bread;* such as he had most obliged, his very Favourites, as he complained (*Psal.* 41. 9 and *Psal.* 55. 13), where he bemoans his own present distress, and the perfidiousness of his own principal Servants and Councellors, who, with Absalom, sought his Life and Crown: Nay they suffered him not to die in peace; for *Adonijah*, another of his darling sons, obtrudes himself a Successor upon him, without his consent or knowledge, and as it were to bury him alive (1 *Kin.* 1. 5, 6).

Thus was this excellent *King* used. And though he left behind him a Successor, a glorious type of Christ, *Solomon*, the wisest King that ever was, or ever will be; yet he fared little better.

He was himself the *wonder*, and made his people the *envy* of the world, by the affluence of all temporal blessings; they had *silver and gold as stones* (2 *Chro.* 1. 15), they were multiplied as the *sand of the sea, eating and drinking, and making merry* (1 *Kin.* 4. 20), a state of life one would think that no discontent could lodge with. But *peace* and *plenty*, which are thought to make men *happy*, cannot always make them *quiet* and *content;* nor can any benefits though never so great, stop the mouth of ingratitude and impatience.

While all the world thought them the happiest people under the Heaven, they murmur and complain at I know not what imaginary *burdens*, which they call *heavy*, and a *grievous yoke* (1 *Kin.* 12. 4), and so little to be endured, that they were ready to break out into Rebellion against him, had not God's mercy and his mercy prevented it, even in his time : And he no sooner dead, but ten tribes, for that reason, cast off the Government of his son, with what success we all know.

But these two, *David* and *Solomon*, had their faults, and great ones too, for which they were punished ! 'Tis true, they had so ; but none to provoke their people to disobedience ; they were private and Personall, not of public concernment ; their Government was just and moderate, never taxed by God as their faults were ; and if this must be assigned a just cause of disturbance, that they were *Governed by Men* not by *Angels*, by those subject to humane infirmities like themselves, all the world would be in a combustion, and none left to govern in peace.

But what say you then (in the last place) to Moses. Innocency it self, one against whom nothing could be justly objected, either as a private or publick person ? sure he must needs escape the malice and machinations of all male contents ! No, he did not ; his condition as bad as any. 'Twas *Moses* I mean ; So rare a person, that (as *St. Ambrose*) *he blotted out all that was man in him by the purity of a conversation*

P

wholly celestiall. And *Josephus* tells us, *that his affections were so governed by wisdome, that he seemed utterly to want them, & that he knew only the names of those persons, which he perceived to be too active in other men.* Most certain it is, that he was an excellent *person* in himself, and an excellent *Governor* to them : I cannot insist upon his particular Vertues in either kind ; sure I am, he wanted none that might oblige his people to obedience. Yet, besides and above all, what a series of *Miracles* were wrought by God, to give him authority and credit among the people ? And sure all this might have been sufficient to secure his quiet in a Government so poor and burthensome, and such as was impossible for any else to manage without the same miraculous assistance of God.

And yet all this could not do it ; for notwithstanding all these advantages, what a wearisome life did he lead in a continuall succession of *murmurings, mutinies, conspiracies, rebellions* of persons neither few nor mean, and some of his *own blood?* How many faults do they charge him with ? *Ambition, misgovernment,* a design to bring the people out of *Aegypt* to perish in the Wilderness, as if these *wanted graves there,* and these reproaches often repeated : And with a wonderfull strange impudence they call him *Tyrant, a killer of God's people,* for what's that else ? And this more than once or twice (*Numb.* 14 and *Numb.* 16). And though God chose him to that command for his very *Meeknesse* (*Ecclus.* 45. 4), and he was indeed the *meekest man upon the face of the earth* (*Num.* 12. 3), yet he is traduced by them as a *Killer of God's people*, as *a Tyrant;* such is the justice of Rebels. It cannot then be thought strange that any after him should suffer under the like calumny that deserved it as little : For if any way faulty, 'twas in too much Lenity.

Thus you see how impossible it is for Governours to escape these scourges, whether they deserve them or no, whether innocent or guilty.

For if *Moses* the *meekest, David* the *best, Solomon the wisest* of *Kings*, felt the smart of popular murmurings, tumults and rebellions; persons as excellent as ever the world had any, or ever will have ; if they could not escape, what good Prince should forfeit his patience by it? think it strange, or be discouraged at it? Or how dare any mis-judge or censure them for it, as if forsaken of God, because abused by men ? or designed for utter ruine, because under his fatherly correction. Consider who these were, what they did, and what they suffered, and then let him that dare pronounce amisse of any in their case and condition.

'Tis clear then by what has been said, that the *best of Kings* may be *under the Cross*, as much as any, and more than any have been, and certainly wil be so to the world's end; and so will, as much as any, need *deliverance* & shal undoubtedly have it, they especially, they before and above others. For they are *God's peculiar care*, they are his *Officers*, his *Deputies*, his honor is concerned in them, and the preservation of them is the good of many; *Thou art worth ten thousand of us*, say *David's* Subjects to him (2 *Sam.* 18. 3).

But though *delivered* they shall be, and ever will be, yet 'tis not always at the same time; some continue longer under the Cross, some are eased sooner: Nor in the same manner and way; some he preserves and supports *in danger*, and at last gives them safety and peace; others he delivers *from danger*, by taking them to himself. The first was the Deliverance of the *three Children*, when they came untouch'd out of the fire; the second of the *Maccabees*, and thousands more, whom by a glorious *Martyrdom* he took to himself. Great Deliverances both, but that of the *Maccabees* much the greater, much the better; when from a fading Crown, a Scepter clouded with cares, and a troublesome Life ever tending to Death, they are delivered up to a Crown of Glory, and a Life Eternal in the Heavens. He that looks not on this as the better of the two, deserves neither; and one of the two they, and all his Servants, may be sure of. So that let *the troubles of the righteous be many & great*, as indeed *many and great* they usually are, yet first or last, one way or the other, and ever to his best advantage, *the Lord delivers him out of all* (*Psal.* 34. 18). And so I pass from the *Person* here *delivered,* to the *Lord that delivered him,* the second thing proposed to your consideration.

II. THAT *all Deliverance comes from* (him, from) *the Lord* 'twere needless to multiply Proofs out of *Scriptures,* which are but the Registers of his *Providence,* and you cannot look besides them there. And 'tis no lesse apparent unto *Reason;* for that (*with great clearness, and by a degree of evidence even beyond knowledge,* as those old Philosophers *Hermes* and *Iamblicus* express it) finds that *there is a God,* and from thence (with as great evidence) demonstrates a *Providence.* So that should I lead you out of the *Church* into the *Schools* of *Philosophers, Poets, Historians,* Writers of all sorts among the Heathens, you would finde them, by the very instinct and impression of Nature, acknowledging the same truth ; ever ascribing all good successes to their *Gods,* and accordingly giving thanks, offering sacrifices, instituting Feasts and Holydayes, putting Garlands upon their Images, leaving part of their spoils taken in their Temples : a Truth so visible, that even blind Nature saw it.

But to our great shame and greater grief be it spoken, we have some among us (I hear many) more heathenish than the Heathen, that will not allow *God* to govern in his own House, that deny him any *care of things below;* so far from delivering us out of danger, that **he** neither regards how we come in, or how we get out, nor at all looks after any thing else we are concern'd in a perswasion extremely cross to the *common notions* of mankind, and impressions of *Nature*, that wholly makes void and ridiculous the duty we are about, and indeed all other; for 'tis totally *destructive* of all *Vertue*, Religion, and *Government*, none of which can possibly subsist, without a belief, a sense, a reverence of some *Divine Power* that will be sure to call for an account of whatsoever we do. Yet they say, these are the *great Wits* of the time, the onely men of parts among us. I wonder at it; 'twas not so thought of old; the language of the *Psalmist* elsewhere imports not any great esteem of them; Nay, he is so far from it, that he wonders at their *sottishness: O ye bruitish among the people & ye fools, when wil ye be wise?* (*Ps.* 94. 8). He speaks of such as when they do wickedly, say; *Tush, the Lord shall not see, neither shal the God of Jacob regard it* (*v.* 7). He wil neither *take notice*, nor *punish*, he looks after nothing here below, we may do what we please for Him. Now let who will admire them, yet these are the men he cals *bruits* and *fools*, and he doth it not once or twice, but very oft. *The fool hath said in his heart, There is no God* (*Ps.* 14. 1), that is, no *Judge*, no *Providence*, (as the word there signifies). And again (*Psal.* 53. 1), and oft elsewhere, if not in the same words, yet to the same sense and purpose. I hope you will not think the term uncivil, 'tis not mine, but *David's*. And if you doubt whether they deserve it, you shall have it from a *wiser* than he, & I hope one they will *acknowledge wiser* than themselves too, even from *Solomon*, who being the wisest of all men, might have the priviledge to be bold with them, as one that best knew what they were; yet he brings them in wondering at the reward of the Righteous, which they believed little of, and putting upon themselves that scorn and title, *We fools counted his life madness* (*Wisd.* 5. 4). We thought ourselves *wise* in pursuing pleasure without check or restraint, and made him *mad* for not doing as we did: but now we finde (too late indeed) but find it we do, and that to our confusion and horror, that his *Madness* was *Wisdom;* and our *Wisdom folly; We fools* thought so, but *Fools* we were, for so thinking. Now what *fools* say is little to be regarded; the sun shines though the blind see it not, and *a God* and *Providence* there is that sends *Deliverance*, though the *fool* say, There is not: and so let the *Atheist* passe under *David's* and *Solomon's* Character, while we to our great comfort (one of the greatest we are capable of in this world) acknowledge, believe, and visibly see, and by experience find, That there is a good *Providence* over us that orders all the affairs of the world from the least to the greatest; from *Empires* and *Thrones to the falling of a Sparrow on the ground, and the*

very numbring of our hairs, as our Saviour
(*S. Math.* 10. 29, 30).

That as 'tis He, and He only, that brings us
into danger, that lays afflictions on us for our
sins; (for *who gave Jacob for a spoil, and Israel to
the robbers?　Did not the Lord, he against whom
they had sinned?　For they would not walk in
his ways, neither were they obedient to his Law,*
therefore *he hath poured upon them the fury of
his anger, and the strength of battel* (*Isa.* 42. 24,
25).　Just our case, we served him so, he served
us so ; our great sins brought his great judgements
upon us.　And) so againe 'tis He, and He onely,
that must remove those afflictions, that must deliver out of those dangers : For, *who is God but the
Lord? and who hath any strength* to doe it *except
our God?*　'Tis *David's* question at ver. 31 of
this *Psalm*, and our answer must be, None can
do it else, none but he: Neither *Men*, nor
Angels, nor any nor all the *Creatures* of Heaven
and Earth can give it.　They may be *Instruments*
in his hand, which he moves, directs, orders,
limits and restrains, when he will and how he
will; he delivers them when he will, no *Means*
too weak with him, none strong enough without
him ; but whether with or without *means*, 'tis still
he that does it, he that delivers, and none else ;
For *the help that is done upon Earth, he doth it
himself*, as 'tis in the Old Translation (*Psal.* 74.
13).

Sure I am, we found it so ; all we did, or could

do, toward a settlement proved nothing worth, all attempts vain, no *Treaties*, no *Armies*, no *Endeavors* by our selves or others that wished well to our Peace did us good, though never so probable, never so hopeful ; they were all lost and frustrate, all vanished into nothing. How visible was God's hand in it, when all rash and unreasonable *attempts* prospered with some, while others failed in the best and most probable? And either the *worst Counsels* were followed (as it usually happens when God determines to judge and afflict a sinfull Nation) or the *best* never prospered, but when brought to ripeness miscarried in the birth. Thus it constantly was, and thus it would have been till we had been utterly consumed, had not he had mercy on us, had not he raised up a *Deliverer*, never to be mentioned without Honour, nor to be forgotten in the *Prayers* of all good People, that God would multiply his favours and blessings, both temporal and spiritual, upon his *Person* and *Posterity* for many generations.

But whoever were the Instruments of our *deliverance*, we must still remember to raise up our thoughts to him by whose power they wrought it, and give him the glory of all ; since nothing is more certain that none did it, none could do it but he ; and having this experience of his power and goodness, it must be a warning to us hereafter, that we loose not our labour in seeking it elsewhere ; that we have patience to wait for it till he is pleased to give it; that we suffer not our eager desires or fears to hasten it, by unlawful means, to purchase it by sin.

Were we right *in our Faith*, we should think it impossible to be had without him (as indeed it is, unless he permit it for our greater mischief; for who can *resist his will?*) and were we right in our *Wits*, we should not think it worth the having, but by him; for he that to escape *Danger*, runs into a *sin*, is much like the starting Horse, who to avoid a *shadow* upon one side the way, leaps down a *precipice*, to his ruine, on the other, and like him that for fear of a lesser, runs into a greater mischief: and to avoid a *Pot-gun* throws himself into the mouth of a *Cannon*. A sad bargain it is, let the *State-Atheist* think what he will, to buy deliverance from the greatest *temporal mischief*, by the least *wilfull sin;* to save Wealth, Honour, Crowns and Scepters, Life it self, any thing we have, or all, at the loss of our God, at the expence of our Soul, which exceeds the whole World in value, and all it hath in it.

But there is a further degree of *Folly* in this course, still a greater blindness; for we sacrifice the comforts of this Life, and hopes of a better, (which every wilful known sin robs us of) for just *nothing:* We believe indeed we purchase *deliverance* by *sin*, and think we have it, when at the best 'tis but an *exchange* of danger, and that too the little for the great; some trouble here, for eternal damnation hereafter: Nay 'tis

ıst not
l that
ıay
.f it.

not always, not oft so much neither, as an *exchange*
of danger, (though that bargain is made sad
enough by the disproportion) but a *doubling* of
it if you will; a contracting a new *danger* by a
new *sin*, and but a running from the old *one way*,
to meet it *another;* a bringing of what we labour
to avoid, with more speed and greater certainty
upon us.

Would you have Resolution of a *Council* of
State-Atheists in the case, and see how it sped?
You shall find it at the 11 *chap.* of St. *John's*
gospel (vers. 47, 48), *What do we?* (say the
Priests and *Pharisees* sitting in Council against
our Saviour) *for this man doth many miracles,
and if we let him alone, all men will believe on
him, and the Romans shall come and take away
both our place and Nation.*

What was resolved on? What was done upon
this? Why the fear of this *danger* put them
upon a horrid *sin*, the shedding of most innocent
blood, they murdered him : And did that avoid
the danger they feared by it? No; the *Romans*
did come, and for the punishment of that very
sin, *took away their place*, carried them captive,
destroyed their *Nation.* 'Tis St. *Augustine's* observation, confirmed by the experience of all ages.

I will not say it always happens so; a speedy
Repentance may sometimes give a stop to the
ordinary course of God's *Judgements;* but it is
very oft, it most commonly happens so, as all
Histories witness, and our own *Experience* can

tell us, perhaps in our own particular affairs; in the *Publick* it hath ever been too visible, when *Reason* of State is opposed to *God, prudence* (falsely so called) and cunning, to *Justice* and *honesty.* For when we begin once to distrust that God cannot, or will not *provide* for our safety, and fall to shift for our selves by such ways as he approves not, we forfeit our title to his good *providence,* (which one way or other would most certainly save us, did we depend upon it) and bring upon our selves the sad effects of distrust, by *changing* our *probable fears* into *certain. sufferings,* and very oft into the same we run from; for we very seldome do wickedly to prevent a mischief, but that very mischief falls upon us, as a punishment for that wickedness. A hundred instances might be given out of Story, and most men's breasts would be found Registers of this sad Truth, would they be pleased to search them well: so clear is that of the *Preacher.* That *wickedness shall not deliver those that are given to it* (*Eccles.* 8. 8).

And therefore if we do indeed believe this most certain truth, *That all deliverance is from the Lord,* we must shew the fruits of that *Faith* when in distresse. And if we cannot by good wayes compasse our safety, never strive to do it by ill; but submit, and expect with *patience* till he is pleased to give it: For then, and not till then, 'twill be a *Deliverance,* indeed. We must not run to the Creature for relief in *dangers but to him;* nor expect *deliverance*, but from Him, nor seek it but in his way, by him, and at his time : And when we have it, to be sure with *David* to *thank* him for it, to pay our Tribute where it is due. And so I passe to the last particular proposed, *David's thankfulnesse for his Deliverance. I will give thanks unto thee (O Lord) among the Heathen, and sing praises unto thy Name.*

III. You have had the *Person delivered,* and *He that delivered him;* now follows the *Duty to be performed upon the deliverance :* Where we may observe,

1. *The person performing it,* that's *David :* I *will,* do it, saith he.

2. *The Duty it self,* that's *Thanksgiving :* I *will give thanks.*

3. *The Manner how* he will do it, and that is,

i. *Publickly,* diffusively not only in the Church, but *among the Heathen* too ;

ii. *Chearfully, I will sing praises.*

Something of each of these in the order proposed. And first of the *Person.*

1. I *will* (sayes *David*) and good reason he should, *He* in the first place, He to lead the way, to give the example. The blessings were *publick,* and he a publick *person,* so more concerned in them than any other, yet others concerned too as well as he, though not so much, even in those *Dangers* that aimed only at his *person :* For that being of *publick concernment,* his *Dangers* and *Deliverances* could be no less : As the *Members* for the

3. Davi thankfu

The Pe: I will.

Head, hurt that, and all suffer with it, even the lowest, the meanest, the mischief descends to all and every one, deliver that from danger, and all rejoyce with it, all the better for it, so that if the *King* have cause to *give thanks*, if he say *I will* do it, all and every one of his subjects must do it too.

'Tis a great shame and folly too, as well as a great sin, so to mind our private as if we had no relation to the *publick;* no Obligation to mourn for, to endeavour to remove *National calamities;* or to *give thanks* and rejoyce for publick Mercies and Deliverances, since the *publick* interest is each *particular's;* for *Quod examini expedit, idem api;* What's good for the *whole*, is good for every *part:* And therefore we should be as *thankfull* for *common blessings*, as if they were bestowed onely upon us; since we have our full share in them, and in our proportion as much as any. To instance in that which most concerns us; *peace* is a collection of all temporal blessings, and that's *Omnium* toto & *singulorum*, every one hath it as much as any, as much as all: Every one hath by it a comfortable and quiet enjoyment of all that belongs to him, every one hath His person and relations secured from violence, his fortune from rapine; and though He have not so much perhaps as others, yet his *All* is as much to him as all theirs to them; and these blessings are as full to thee, as if thou onely enjoyedst them; and more to thy *Security*, be-

cause others injoy them with thee. And therefore since *every Man* is concerned in the *Benefit*,
every man must betake himself to the *Duty*;
that's *Thankfulness. I will give thanks.* The
next particular.

2. And here the time is very observable: The Du
Our *Prophet* was no sooner *delivered*, but he "Give
made a right use of that blessing, he fell to
his Duty of *Thanks* for it; a thing not so
usuall, either with Kings or meaner persons.
For if any disturbance intermit our sinfull
pleasures, no sooner that over, but we return
to them again, and with more greediness.
David will not do it; Now (saith he) I see
the tempest over, the clouds dispersed, my
troubles at an end, shall I wanton it as before?
No, I will give thanks unto thee, O Lord.

And this example speaks our duty; for as *he*
did, so must *we:* In ill we follow *Kings* fast
enough, tread upon their heels, if not out-go
them; their example works much upon us, too
much; why not in Vertue; why not something
at least that way? In a *duty* so necessary it
should, a *Duty* we cannot avoid without great
sin as here we cannot. For *Gratitude* is an
act of *Justice*, the paying of a debt, and no
part of *Justice* more necessary, even to preserve the very frame of *Nature* and *humane
society*, which subsist by nothing more, nothing
else, but a mutuall exchange of good offices;
take away these, the whole world and all in it

must perish; for no Man can live of himself, nor can any thing subsist of it self, there must be a mutual gratitude and exchange of offices to preserve all.

But the subject is infinit, should we take it at large; we must restrain it to the present occasion, and follow *David's* steps as close as we can; his case was much like ours; we equal'd him in danger, let's match him in thankfulnesse; in him great *blessings*, and great *thanks* met well together; we come not behind in *mercy*, let's not fall short in *gratitude*. Do it we must, and do it to the full we should; that our *Thankfulness* may in some measure (at least as far as our ability will carry us) answer his great *bounty;* since, where much is given, there's not a little required. We have his *promise* indeed, for *deliverance* out of *danger*, but 'tis usher'd in with one *command* to *ask* it, and followed with another to be *thankfull for it* (*Psal.* 50. 15). *Call upon me in the time of trouble* (there's the command to ask it) *and I will hear thee*, (there's the promised deliverance; for his hearing is delivering :) *And thou shalt praise me;* there's the duty enjoyned. The two first are passed with us, God be thanked for it. We *prayed*, we *asked*, we *called;* he *heared*, he *delivered*. Now remains our duty, our *praise and thanksgiving.*

uty

A small Tribute, God knows; a *duty* so *easie*, nothing can excuse us from it. Other duties want not excuses, have some just impediments

in some persons, and at some times; as *poverty,
impotency, sickness,* or the like; this hath none,
can have none; All may do it, and at any time;
the rich and the poor, the sick and the well, the
lame and the sound: He that wants not an heart,
though he want all things else, though a tongue,
may yet *give thanks* and *praise; Ipsum voluisse,
landasse est; non enim verba quærit, sed cor.*
(Aug. in *Psal.* 134). When all other ways of
expressing our thanks fail us, if *sincerely,* and in
earnest we *would* do it, we have done it.

And as what he requires is *easie,* so 'tis *little,* 2 Little.
very little; *little in itself,* what can be less than
Thanks; but compared with his great mercies,
then this *little* is just nothing. The Patriarch
Jacob confessed to God, that he was *less than the
least of his Mercies* (*Gen.* 32. 10). Yet he a *Gyant*
in vertue and worth, we, the best of us, but *Pigmies*
to him; and if *He* (as great as he was) *were less
then the least:* What are we to his *great mercies,*
but just *nothing.*

Yet such poor wretches we are, 'tis *All* we
have for him, *All* we can return to him; and
if he will have *any thing,* he must have this
nothing. And so gratious he is, that he calls
for it, he accepts it, he is content with this
nothing, such as it is: Requires no more from
us, than *thanks* and *praise;* and a great vouch-
safement it is, that he will suffer us to do it, so
great and glorious he, so vile and despicable we';
yet he will have it, he is pleased with it.

Q

But that too for *us*, not for *himself;* we gain
by it, not *he;* 'tis nothing to *him*, much to *us;*
he is neither the better, if we *thank him*, nor
the worse if we *thank him not;* whether we
praise or dispraise him, he is still the same;
but we are both, better or worse, as we
do it, or neglect it; 'tis ever better with us
when we do it, worse when we do it not.
Cast any thing up toward Heaven, it falls down
upon thee again; send up *thanks* and *praise*, and
they descend in new *favors* and *blessings;* send
them not up, and look for no more; *Accipiendis
indignus, qui de acceptis ingratus*, (Bern). Nay
look to lose those thou hast, for be sure they will
wither and come to nothing; either they will be
taken away, or if they stay, they shall not minister
comfort, not *that very comfort* which in their own
nature they seem to bring; they are not, they
shall not be *blessings* to thee; the *comfort* is gone,
and that's not all; they turn to *curses*, become
aggravations of *sin*, additions to judgement: Such
a wretched change doth *unthankfulness* make.

Do but observe how uneasie some men are in
the affluence of all earthy blessings, how froward,
how discontent, how little joy they take in them?
(and *God* grant it be not many a man's case
amongst us, and even in the enjoyment of our
present blessings,) examine the cause, search the
root of this mischief, and 'twill be found nothing
but *Ingratitude* to *God* for them; who though he
leaves the *things* themselves, yet takes away the

blessing, the joy, the comfort of them. And who can say, but that a slight esteem, a negligent acknowledgment of his great favors, deserves all this?

Since then this duty of *praise* and *thanks* is so profitable, if we do it; so mischievous, if we do it not; since we are happy, if we do it (for do that, and God will do the rest: Continue to multiply his *blessings* upon us, preserve what we have, and give more, even more than we need, more than we ask;) and on the other side we are utterly undone, if we do it not; for then there is no keeping of what we have, or if the *thing* stay by us, the *blessing* of it will be taken from us, and we shall be as miserable in Peace, and much more than we were in war. And as we cannot *keep* what we *have*, so we cannot *hope* for what we *want*: Our *Ingratitude* hath stopped the passage, dryed up the Fountain of his Mercies towards us, all our hopes are at an end.

And the case being thus, 'tis most necessary that our next enquiry be, *What this duty of thankfulnesse is*, and how we may discharge our selves of it as we ought.

Gratitude in its general notion, is that vertue Gratitud by which we make some convenient or fitting return to another, for some free benefit received from him, and the several *acts, parts*, or *duties* of it, are three.

1. *To acknowledge the benefit.*
2. *To thank and praise the Benefactor.*

3. *To repay him with the like, or some other kindness, as our ability will serve and opportunity is offered.*

So that 'tis in the *mind* first; then in the *mouth*, both full of *praise* and *thanks;* yet the duty not full, untill it fill the *hands* too ; *conceived* it must be in the *heart, declared* it must be by the *tongue, perfected* it must be by the *hand:* And that all these may do their parts, we will a little consider them apart.

the

1. And first, the root of this lies in the *heart,* the *fountain* of every good action : *Gratitude* must begin there, by an inward acknowledgment and just esteem of the benefit received; not to acknowledge, or deny it, is an impudent piece of *Ingratitude;* to forget it, base ; and to under-value it, comes not far behind either. All these sins, I fear, we have much to answer for; and such as brought our late judgments upon us. Now a *just estimate* of what we have received, is a remedy against all these : For if we find that great, especially in any high measure, we cannot for shame, either *deny, undervalue,* or *forget* it ; and therefore, that we may do our duty in the business we are met about, our main, first, and chiefest work must be, to fix upon our *hearts* a *due esteem,* a true sense of the worth and value of the *great blessing* we have lately *received* from *God,* and are here met to pay our *thanks* for; and the best measure of it is taken from the consideration.

1. *Of the Giver.*
2. *The benefit it self.*
3. *The manner of giving.*
4. *The time when.*
5. *And the persons upon whom bestowed.*

All or any of which use either to heighten or lessen a benefit received.

1. And first, the *Giver* commends the gift; the hand it comes from, adds value to it: a little favor from an great person is ever much esteemed; a small Donative from a *Prince*, more valued than greater matters from an *ordinary person.* And there is reason for it; for, besides the *honor* we get with *others* to be so valued by those of high esteem, it brings *satisfaction* and *comfort* to *our selves*, especially in our present case between *God* and us, to have such an assurance, such an earnest of his good will, who is able to do so much for us: It lets us out into new expectations of receiving still more and more, from a bounty so great, so lasting, so boundless, so endless. Indeed, *between men* the difference though much, cannot be so much to heighten the benefit; not more than between one piece of earth and another, the *Mountain* and the *Molehill* at the most; but in the comparison between *God and us*, we shall be utterly astonished, utterly lost; that *he* so great, so glorious, so infinite in all perfections, beyond all we can say or think; should yet vouchsafe to look down upon *us*, to be kind to *us*, so poor,

1. A du esteem c the Give

so weak, so vile, so despicable Creatures, even nothing, and worse than nothing in comparison of him. What a condescention is this in him? What an *honor* and *comfort* to us? How much doth it commend any favour, even the least, to be an earnest of so infinite a bounty? And therefore in all such cases our *gratitude* must not arise so much from the solace that *nature* finds in any *blessing* bestowed upon us, as from the consideration of the bounty and goodness of so infinite a *Majesty* towards us.

2. Thus you see the *Giver* is great, greater than all givers else put together, great beyond compare. What is in the next place, the *Gift* it self? That's great too; and though all are so that come from him, yet some are greater than others, and this in its kinds as great as any, both in respect of the mischiefs we are delivered from, and the *Blessings* we receive by it. There's no descending to particulars on either side, they are infinite, easie it is to begin to speak of the one, or the other; the *Miseries of War*, or the *Blessings of Peace:* But we know not where to end, since both are innumerable; and the bare names of *War* and *Peace*, carry to every man's understanding a summary, a collection of all temporall *mischiefs* and *blessings*. And if there be any in Heaven or Hell upon Earth, these are they, and the distance as great; however, they are excellent Hieroglyphicks of both; no two things in the world resemble them better.

So that if we consider what we have escaped, the *miseries of War*, and of a *Civil War*, the worst of all wars; and what we have gained, the *blessings of Peace*, and *Kingly Government* the best preserver of them; a gracious PRINCE, and together with him our *Laws, Liberties, Properties*, the *free exercise of Religious Duties*, indeed all that is or ought to be dear to a Christian Common-wealth in this world: if we consider I say what he hath removed from us, and what he hath given to us, the Blessings will appear in it *self* wonderfull; and in its kind, beyond compare.

3. And yet his *Love* and *Liberality* in the manner of bestowing it, is as wonderful as the *gift* it self, and more; and that in a double respect. For first, he did it graciously, freely, *Nullo antecedente merito, nullo expectato commodo;* he saw nothing in us before to move him to it; he looks for nothing after from us for it, but onely that we should be kinde to our selves in a right use of his benefits; that so we may be capable of more and greater, which we long not so much to receive, as he to give. And

3. Of the Manner giving it

Secondly, Because what he gives in *frowns* and *thunder* to others, he hath reached out to us *smiling*, and in his *still voice*, what they *buy* by all the miseries of War, and think it a good purchase oft at the expence of much treasure, and a sea of Blood, is freely cast upon us without more cost or trouble than a few *Concessions* of a *gracious Prince;* now so great a *blessing* at so easie a rate, so much for so little, must needs highly commend his bounty, and make the *manner of his giving equal* to the *gift* it self.

4. And as the *Manner most gracious*, so was the *Time* too. A little thing seasonably done, deserves much : This was great in it *self*, gracious in the *manner*, seasonable for the *time;* 'tis danger that makes *deliverance* sweet. *Placet cunctis securitas, etc.*, says St. *Bernard*, security is pleasing to all, but to him most that feared most; and to be snatched out of the jaws of *Death*, gives a double *Life*. This was our case ; *rescued*, when ready to *perish*, when *Church* and *State*, *Religion*, *Learning*, *Laws*, were not only in danger, but already devoured, in the hope and expectation of our enemies ; when *Atheism*, *Ignorance*, and *Barbarism*, were in a full and fierce torrent, breaking in upon us, and we at the very brink of a remediless confusion, ready to be made the pity and scorn of the whole world, as they stood affected to us ; *Then*, even *then*, in this pressing necessity, at this most acceptable *Time*, did the day begin to break, and his mercy to shine upon us ; then we first discerned our *deliverance* dawning, which, by several gracious steps and degrees, he hath since wonderfully perfected.

5. And as a *Time* most seasonable for our necessities, so, to make the mercy on all hands compleat, at a *Time* too, when we seemed *most uncapable of it*, most *unworthy of it :* For who, or what were we, that such a blessing should be

cast upon us? not only *undeserving*, but *ill deserving*, and that in a high measure; most worthy to be utterly *consumed*, most unworthy to be *preserved*: And you know the less worth in the *Receiver*, ever the more favour in the *Giver*. But to take a right esteem of our selves, we may do wel to consider,

1. *What our condition was before these Judgments fell upon us.*

2. *What under them.*

3. *What at the time of our deliverance from them.*

1. At first, *Blessings* we had so *many*, so *great*, as no Nation under Heaven enjoyed *more* or *greater*: But did we grow the better by them? were we thankful for them? Far from it; God knows we forgot many, undervalued more, abused all. In stead of the fruits of so great a bounty, nothing to be seen among us but horrid impudent sins; *Non furtiva scelera sed in publicum misse* (as the *Stoick* of his time;) not sneaking, private, concealed sins, as fearing the *Laws* or *shame* of the *World;* but *open, publick*, and *National sins;* Drunkenness, Reeling in the streets, Blasphemy sounding in the Market-place, Perjury in Courts of Justice, Churches themselves not free, Pride and Oppression, Luxury and Prophaneness, Lust and Uncleanness, and what not? But above all, our base *Ingratitude* amidst the greatest Blessings, ever restless and impatient, complaining of the Times, and murmuring at those under whose blessed Government we enjoyed them with so great

1. Wha condition was befc our trou

security. Our own hearts must needs witness against us, That the accusation is most just; and 'tis not a time to trifle with ourselves, to palliate and extenuate our *sins*, but freely and fully to confess them, if we mean not to make void his present *Mercies*, and pull yet greater *Judgments* upon us. This sin made us think our *Peace* a *burden*, and gave us no quiet till we had thrown away those inestimable blessings; and for want of other Enemies, with our own hands pull mischief upon our selves, mutually scourging and afflicting one another by all the miseries of a bloudy, civil and unnatural War : And thus came his Judgments upon us.

And now to proceed.

2. When *Gideon* returned from the pursuit of the two Kings of *Midian*, and had *torn the men of Succoth and Penuel with the thorns and bryers of the Wildernesse*, 'tis said, that with them he *taught the men of Succoth* (Judg. 8. 16), because afflictions and punishments use to do it, use to *teach* men *Wit* and *Vertue*, use to restrain them from their wicked courses. Did our mutual *tearing* of one another's flesh *teach us?* Had it so good an effect upon us ? Alas no : we grew not better, but worse by it; our *sins* multiplied with, and much beyond our *sufferings*, especially *Atheism, Prophanenesse, Sacriledge, Perjury, Oppression, innocent Blood* of all Degrees, *Vulgar, Noble, Sacred*, and *Royal;* not to be mentioned without tears of blood to bewail it,

nat
them.

So that when we were come to this height of wickedness; and made our selves the reproach of the whole world, what could we in reason expect, but that the full Vials, and the very dregs of his wrath should be poured down upon us, and we utterly destroyed from the face of the earth?

3. Yet so wonderful was his mercy, even in this state and condition, when our provocations reached up to Heaven, seemed to contend and prevail too, both against his Love and Anger, abusing the one, contemning the other, and profiting by neither; when thus full ripe for destruction, yet, as if he were resolved not to be overcome by our ingratitude, nor suffer any thing to hinder his gracious purposes towards us, he hath, by a *Miracle of Mercy*, removed his Judgments from us, and becalmed that tempest that lay so heavy upon us, what can we do less than cry out with our Prophet, *O that men would therefore praise the Lord for his goodnesse, and declare the wonders that he doth for the children of men* (Psa. 107).

And now if we be not wholly drowned in sensuality, if we be not guilty of a stupidity beyond what humane nature seems capable of, we must needs be highly and passionately sensible of so melting, so surprizing, so amazing a Mercy; so *exceeding great* in all considerations: so great the *Giver*, so vile the *Receivers;* the *Gift* so great, the *Manner* so kind, the *Time* so seasonable, and *We* so *unworthy* of it: what can be more to commend it to us? And therefore, if we have

3. Wha the tim of our Deliver

but near that relish of it in the *heart* as we ought, and as it deserves, it will break out at the *mouth*, and break out it must into *Praise* and *Thanksgiving:* For that was the next part of *David's Gratitude*, and must be so of ours.

> *I will give thanks unto thee, O Lord, and sing praises to thy Name, among the Heathen.*

titude
tongue.

2. If *Gratitude* be in the heart, if all be right within, something will appear without: If there be that apprehension, that estimation of the *blessing* as it deserves, it cannot be kept there no more than fire in the bosome, it will break out in *thanks* and *praise;* the full *heart* will run over at the *mouth*, it must have a vent by the *tongue:* And so indeed it should, both for our own good, and for others too. The *tongue* was principally given (you know) to set forth his *praise* and *glory*, and it concerns us to use it accordingly. We offend with it as much as with any member, and therefore should by it endeavour to make some compensation, and take care it be as serviceable as before sinful. We pull down *Judgments* by it, and 'tis but meet we give *thanks* with it for our *Deliverance;* else we shall be found guilty of *cold affections, dull resentments* of his favours: We rob God of his *Glory*, and others of the benefits of his *Mercies* to us, for whose sakes we receive them as well as for our own; that *they*, as well as *we*, may have comfortable hopes of *Deliver-*

ance, when in distresse ; and learn by our example
to give *Praise* and *Glory* to his Name.

Necessary then it is, that the *Tongue* have 1. Publi
its part in the discharge of this duty ; our
thanks must be *vocal*, and more than that, they
must be *publick* too and *diffusive*. *David* would
not pay them privately, and to a few, but
publickly, even among the *Gentiles* in the *Church*
and without, even to all mankinde. He was a
Prophet, and foresaw the conversion of the *Gentiles*, and that the *Psalm* he composed should be
sung to the *praise* and *glory* of *God* among them,
that his example should minister matter of *thanks*
to all succeeding ages. But I promised not to
meddle with the *Prophetical sense* at all ; the
Literal reacheth far enough to our instruction,
and may suffice to teach us to imitate him in publishing our thanks as he did, who (that none
might be ignorant of his *gratitude*, who had
heard of his *Deliverance*) would do it in *the great
Congregation*, and among much people (*Psal.*
35. 18). He calls to others to assist him, and
joyn with him ; to do it themselves, *Tell the
people what things he hath done* (*Psal.* 105. 1).
*O come hither and hearken, and I will tell you
what he hath done for my soul* (Psal. 66. 16).
And, *O praise the Lord with me, and let us
magnifie his name together* (Psal. 34. 3). *O be
joyful all the Lands ;* and many such like. He
will do it to everybody, that all may praise God
as well as he ; he will not be ashamed, nor should

we, to own and confesse, and acknowledge, and publish his bounty in all places, and before all persons, as occasion and opportunity is offered. A heart truly affected with a sense, and due esteem of his mercy, will do it, cannot forbear to do it, is restless till it have done it. Both *publickly* and *chearfully* too, another circumstance in the manner of giving our *thanks;* of which likewise,

earfully. The *Prophet* gives here an example, for he will not onely say, but *Sing praises unto his Name;* declare a *joyfulness* as well as *thankfulness.* And so it should be, and so it must be. For as to *Feast* when God calls to Fast; to *sing*, when he calls to *sigh*, is in the Prophet, *an iniquity not easily purged (Isai.* 22. 12, 13, 14). (To frolick it under his judgments, and to despise them so much, as not to seem sensible of them, is a great *sin*, and I fear no small part of our former guilt.) So, on the contrary, to carry *sour countenances* when his *shines* upon us, to entertain his mercies with a sullen and sad heart, an unfeeling disposition, or but with an indifference; not to be at all transported, at all moved with them, is a *sin* that deserves a desertion, a recalling of his *favors*, a doubling his *judgments* upon us. A sad example we have in the people of God. *Deut.* 28, 47, 48, *Because thou didst not serve the Lord thy God with joyfulness, and with gladness of heart, for the abundance of all things : Therefore thou shalt serve thine enemies in hunger, thirst, and nakedness, and in the want of all things.* An heavy doom, and the reason of it is; where there is no *joy without*, there can be no *hearty thanks within*. For how can we esteem any thing a *blessing* that *delights* us not? And how are we delighted if we shew no signs of *joy* for it? And how does he value a Deliverance, that expresses no comfort he takes in it? This is certainly a great sin, an high provocation of God? What shall we say then to those sowre and over-leavened natures, that with the same countenance keep a *Fast* and a *Festival*, a day of *Humiliation* and *Thanksgiving*, both alike, with sighs, and groans, and cast down looks; as if *griefs* and *groans* were a certain sign of *Grace* and *Godliness*, when the Devils howl and are tormented.

But I would not be mistaken; 'tis not a *profane rejoycing*, a sinful mirth we plead for; far be it from us: How much those usual expressions of jollity, *singing, feasting*, and the like, are abused to Luxury and Riot, Excess and Wantonness, *Novimus et Dolemus*, (as the Father) we know it, we grieve for it, we detest it as much as any. An horrid sin it is, in stead of *thanking God*, to sacrifice to *Bacchus*; to express *Publicum gaudium per Publicum dedecus*, as *Tertullian* of the Heathen: That's to pay *thanks* with *unthankfulness*, to make *Mercy* the Mother of *Sin*, to return evil for good, the worst, the highest, the basest Ingratitude.

The *corruption* of the *best* things is ever the *worst*, and what's most *necessary* in the *use*, is ever most *dangerous* in the *abuse:* And so 'tis here; abuse *Mirth*, and nothing worse, use it right and nothing better; keep it within its bounds, suffer it not to transport us beyond our duty into sin, and 'tis the *Balm of this Life*, the *Earnest of a better*, the Condiment and seasoning, that which makes pleasant all actions Moral and Religious.

'Tis an excellent Rule of Life St. *Bernard* gives, *Do well and be merry;* as merry as you will, the more the better; keep to the first, you cannot offend in the second. And let me tell you, that *Vertue* and *Religion* are the most *chearfull* things in the World, however some make them sowr and severe; they are, like God himself, all light and serenity, joy and comfort, especially in his service.

God loves the chearful servant, and who does not? We may judge it by our selves. Who cares for him who goes to his *work* as if he went to the *Stocks* or a *Prison?* All parts of God's service, even the sowrest and severest (had we time to shew it) are mixed with comforts, and should be performed joyfully; this of *Thanksgiving* above and beyond, and more than any: For here we swim with the stream. We are naturally chearful after a mischief avoided, a danger escaped; and being so well prepared for it, should with all alacrity *sing* out our *thanks* and his *praise*, declare an exultation of mind in all innocent and decent expressions of joy and gladness.

'Twas ever the custome of all mankind to do it, in all ages and places: Instances are infinite both within the Church and without. But in *David*, who in the Book of *Psalms*, for his several deliverances, is ever at [*I will sing,*] or [*O sing unto the Lord:*] either doing it himself, or calling others to do it, not coldly or faintly, but zealously and heartily; *sing aloud, make a chearfull noise; Sing lustily unto him with a good courage.* But this will not serve the turn neither, unless he call for Instruments, as well as men to assist; *Bring hither the Tabret, the merry Harp, and the Lute, blow the Trumpet too*, all to incite, quicken and enflame his heart and affections, even to a transporting extatic joy of gratitude.

We should indeed labour to foment it in us as much as may be, for the greater *joy without*, the greater *sense* and esteem of his *bounty within;* and the greater that is, ever the more, and the more sincere *gratitude;* which if it be not *heard* in our *Tongues*, is certainly not *felt* in our *Hearts*, and therefore there it must be also.

And when this is done, the second part of gratitude is performed; the *Tongue* hath done her part, but all is not yet done; this is but *gratiarum dictio*, it reacheth no further then *words*, and something must be *done* as well as said.

The *thanks* of some are vocal enough, too much, because nothing else, nothing but sound and noise; and better a dumb heart then not sincere.   Words are a cheap way of payment, and the world delights much in it; God's benefits are not *words*, but *deeds*, and our gratitude will be found short if it reach not beyond words to *deeds*.   Nay, Honesty and Reason require, that the compensation exceed the benefit received, that the return be made both in greater *measure*, and with greater alacrity (if it may be;) Because he that gave was, *not obliged*, he that returns, is; the one comes from a free and liberal *mind*, the other is a piece of *Justice*, and a Debt: And though we have paid what's due to Justice, in returning as much as we received; yet we are not upon even terms, unless we suffer one *kind-nesse* to beget another, and return something over and above, and more then we received.   A good man will do it when he can, and have a good mind, an earnest *desire* to do it when he cannot.   And so should we to God, since 'tis impossible to make him answerable returns in *fact*, we must do it *in voto*, in desire.   And though neither our *deeds* nor *desires* can in any degree equal his Bounty, but we must needs fall infinitely short in both; yet if we do what we can, and heartily wish we could do more, 'tis accepted with him.

And *something* (sure) we can do, and that *something* we must do.   Now to learn what it is, we must consider; why we were *afflicted*, and why *delivered?* afflicted we were for our *sins*, delivered that we might *sin no more*. What those *sins* were that pulled down his *judgments* upon us, you heard before; how many, how great, how publick, how bold and daring; how our *provocations* multiplied with and beyond his *judgments*. And now being delivered, we must remember, that *mercy* is ever shewed *propter spem*, in hope of amendment; and therefore take care to avoid those sins hereafter; at least to be sure to prevent their being publick and national any more.

For if instead of improving this blessing of *Peace* to his glory, the good of others, and of our selves, we abuse it to pride and vanities, pleasure and sensuality, excess and riot, we may be assured it will prove no blessing at all, but an *aggravation*, both of our *guilt* and *misery*, in bringing a worse war, and heavier judgments upon us, then we have yet felt.

But this is not all, we have more to do, to be thankful as we should, then this; then, barely to avoid sin; we must *do good too*. For the general end of all his blessings upon us, his mercies to us, and *deliverance* of us, of what kinde soever, is to lead us to a *holy, vertuous*, and *religious life* (*St. Luk.* i. 74, 75). We are brought into danger and distress, because *bad*, delivered that we may be *better*. And this is the right *giving of thanks*, the best return we can make him, and the best esteemed by him: And so (you see) there` is much more required to make up this duty, then

2. In dc good.

words; much before, and much after, the *heart* before, and after the *hands.* If the first (the *heart*) be wanting, *words* are but *wind,* not better, nor so innocent as the pratling of a Parrot. *Gratitude* is *heartless* without the one, and *lame* without the other. When either is wanting (the *heart* or *hands*) the *Tongue* is an *Hypocrite,* and gives *lies* instead of *thanks;* real thanks are good deeds, and they praise him best, that obey him best.

giving. But now among those many duties a good life comprehends, and we in *gratitude* are obliged unto; some are more seasonable, more proper for this time and occasion. And to make the choice, we shall especially consider, that as *God hath done great things for us,* so it is necessary we *do something* again for him : As he hath *given* to us, so we *to give* to him. Alas, how can that be? since our goods reach not to him, *he* needs them not. True indeed, but *His* do ; the *poor* need, and by them our goods reach even to *Him* too. We relieve him in the *poor,* visit him in the *sick,* cloath him in the *naked,* redeem him in the *prisoner : For in that we do it to these, we do it to him* (*Matth.* 25. 45). And no time more seasonable to do it in, none fitter then this : That at a *publick rejoycing* none may be *sad,* nor *fast* when others *feast :* and therefore, being cheered, refreshed, and comforted our selves, let us cheer, refresh, and comfort others ; and being delivered ourselves, let's deliver others

from distress and want; those especially that
have suffered in the late disturbances, the *sick*,
the *maimed*, the *lame*, the *desolate Widows* and
Children of such as fell in the service. Let's be
sure to make them (as well as ourselves) sensible
of *God's favors* to us : Let the *blessings* of *peace*
distil from the *head* to the *skirts*, to the very
meanest among us : *Works of Charity* are a
proper *sacrifice* of *thanks*giving at such a time
as this.

But besides *giving*, there must be *forgiving* 2. Forgi
too, a duty at this time as seasonable as the
other, if not more ; for it is the best part of our
gratitude to *God*, and the most acceptable to him,
and we shall be without excuse, if we do it not.
For shall God forgive us *Thousands of Talents*,
sins many in number, great in weight? And
shall we stick at a *few pence*, a few petty injuries
of our Brethren, neither great, nor many ; but
such as for *number* or *weight* can stand in no
comparison with ours against him ? Shall *God*,
so great, so glorious, after so high and many
provocations, condescend to be at peace with us,
and give us an assurance of it, by removing his
judgments, and *crowning* us with many *blessings?*
And shall *we* (poor worms) be at enmity among
our selves for trifles, and that to the hazard of
all the *comforts* of this life, and hopes of a better ?
Shall *we* retain the memory of former unkind-
nesses, and make a *Publick Act of Oblivion*,
which we expect a *public lye;* without either

fear of *God*, or shame of the *World?* This is not to *have peace*, or enjoy it ; but with great ingratitude to *throw* it at him again ; it is but to change one war into another, the open into secret, hostility into treachery ; and by pretending *peace* and *kindness*, to smooth the way to *supplantation* and *injury*, the most *base, serpentine, unmanly thing* in the World.

And therefore I beseech you, take care that we strip our selves of all *unruly passions*, that we may have *peace within*, peace from turbulent revengeful affections : For unless we have this, what's *outward peace* worth? Certainly no more to thee then health in the *City*, when the *Plague* is in thy *bosome*. Let's all seriously and sadly look back, consider, and bemoan one another : For what we have mutually done and suffered from each other ; let's all be *sorry* for it, and all *mend*, perfectly *forgiving* what's past, and returning to as great a kindness as ever, and a greater then ever ; that so, by all *mutual good offices* we may make amends for our former *Animosities*.

It hath been our custom indeed and (more shame for us) to *forget benefits*, to write them in *sand*, but injuries in *marble ;* we must now invert the order, write *God's benefits* in marble, others injuries in sand, if we write them at all ; never *forget* the one, never *remember* the other ; that's the best, the most *Christian memory*, which (as *Cæsars*) *forgets* nothing but *injuries :* We should all do it, and *Princes* above all ; for it becomes a *Publick Father*, to look upon all as *sons*, upon the *Prodigals*, with more kindness and tenderness, when they once come to themselves, acknowledge their errors, when he sees them *returning*, though *afar off*, to *run*, and *meet*, and *caress* them; to call for the *Ring* and the *Robe;* to set some marks of favour upon them more than ordinary, that may give assurance to the World and them, that the promises made them, were not the *effects of necessity*, but the *fruits* of a *gracious Princely minde*, inviolably resolved to outdo all his *Promises* and *Engagements*.

Lastly, and to conclude, Let every one of us (I beseech you) think upon these and the like duties, which this time and occasion call for, and continue them at all times. *Gratitude* is not the business of a day or a year, but of our *whole life. Benefits* new and fresh, are usually entertained by us with *warm affections*, but (more shame for us) a little time cools them, deads them : And *dangers* are too oft at once past and forgotten; or if we set apart a time, a *Day of Thanksgiving* (as now we do) when that is past, commonly our thanks pass with it, and we return to our old vanities again. *David* does not so, he gives a better example; he says, *I will give thanks*, I will *begin*, (and indeed he had begun before he said it) but he says not when he will *end*, he sets no time for that; nor could he, because it should have none, it should be without end : And therefore elsewhere he is at it; *Every day will I give thanks*

2. By persevering in both.

unto thee, and praise thy Name for ever and ever, (*Psal.* 145. 2). 'Tis *indecent* and indeed *unjust,* our *Thanks* should be *transitory,* when the *Benefit* is *lasting.* Now that, (if we forfeit it not by unthankfulness) lasts as long as wee ; we are, and ever shall be, the better for it ; For had we perished in the danger, we had utterly lost the benefit of this and all succeeding Mercies. Our *Thanks* then should last as long as it lasts, and that's as long as we last, and must not end before us. And therefore let every one of us, as we are obliged, take up *David's* resolution and practise, and say with him, *Praise the Lord, O my soul; while I live will I praise the Lord, as long as I have any being will I sing praise unto my God* (*Psal.* 146. 1). And thus *saying,* and thus *doing,* we shall continue those Blessings upon us, which may make this and succeeding Generations happy. Which God, &c.

[This Sermon, delivered at the rate of sixty words a minute, must have taken from three to four hours in preaching !—V. S.]

APPENDIX V

INSCRIPTION ON SHELDON'S TOMB IN CROYDON CHURCH

Fortiter et Suaviter.

HIC JACET
GILBERTUS SHELDON
ANTIQUA SHELDONIORUM FAMILIA
IN AGRO STAFFORDIENSI NATUS,
OXONII
BONIS LITERIS ENUTRITUS.
S. S^{TAE} THEOLOGIÆ DOCTOR INSIGNIS ;
COLL : OMNIUM ANIMARUM CUSTOS PRUDENS ET FIDELIS,
ACADEMIÆ CANCELLARIUS MUNIFICENTISSIMUS,
REGII ORATORII CLERICUS,
CAR I^{MO} B. MARTYRI CLARISSIMUS ;
SUB SERENISSIMO R. CAROLO II^{DO},
MDCLX, MAGNO ILLO INSTAURATIONIS ANNO,
SACELLI PALATINI DECANUS,
LONDINIENSIS EPISCOPUS ;
MDCLXII, IN SECRETIONIS CONCILII ORDINEM
COOPTATUS ;
MDCLXIII. AD DIGNITATIS ARCHIEPISCOPALIS APICEM
EVECTUS.
VIR
OMNIBUS NEGOCIIS PAR, OMNIBUS TITULIS SUPERIOR,
IN REBUS ADVERSIS MAGNUS, IN PROSPERIS BONUS,
UTRIUSQUE FORTUNÆ DOMINUS ;
PAUPERUM PARENS
LITERATORUM PATRONUS,
ECCLESIÆ STATOR.
DE TANTO VIRO
PAUCA DICERE NON EXPEDIT, MULTA NON OPUS EST ;
NORUNT PRÆSENTES, POSTERI VIX CREDENT
OCTOGENARIUS
ANIMAM PIAM ET CŒLO MATURAM
DEO REDIDIT
V. ID. IX. B^{RIS}
MDCLXXVII.

INDEX

WELLS GARDNER, DARTON & CO. LTD

THE LIBRARY LIST.

The Best Biographies.

CHARLES EDWARD BROOKE.
A Memoir.

5s. net.

Edited by **Arthur Gordon Deedes**, Vicar of St. John the Divine, Kennington; Hon. Canon Southwark.
With an Introduction by **Lord Halifax**.

The late Canon Brooke was perhaps the finest example of a man of advanced views who yet was beloved and respected by all who differed even vitally from him. He was virtually the builder and endower of S. John's, Kennington; and his public services included long membership of the London School Board. He was a master of organization, and his parish was probably the best 'run' in England. One who disagreed with him on most points wrote that if ' he himself ever got to Heaven, he would be thankful if he was allowed a place at Mr. Brooke's feet.'

Extract from Lord Halifax's Introduction :—
'Charles Edward Brooke was one of those who make goodness attractive. He was a thorough Englishman. . . . It is well that such a witness should be borne to his external work. . . . It is still better that the memory of such a life should be invested with all the permanence we can bestow upon it.'

WILLIAM DALRYMPLE MACLAGAN,

Bishop of Lichfield, afterwards Archbishop of York.

By **F. D. How**.

With four Photogravures and other Illustrations. **16s.** net.

[*Second Edition.*

Affairs of more than usual importance are included in this history of a life which was in itself a revelation of a noble personality.

'A man full of grace.'
WESTMINSTER GAZETTE

'A valuable contribution to the history of the Church in the nineteenth century.' **DAILY MAIL.**

'I REMEMBER.'

Memories of a 'Sky Pilot' in the Prison & the Slum.

[*Second Edition.*

By **John William Horsley**, Hon. Canon of Southwark.

7s. 6d. net.

Canon Horsley is well known as a vigorous social reformer, an exhilarating and endlessly amusing speaker, and a hard, untiring worker in all good causes. His striking personality is impressed on every page of this brightly-written book, which cannot fail to interest.

'An exceptional biography.'
MORNING POST.

'Not only interesting, but stimulating and suggestive.'
TELEGRAPH.

A SHEPHERD OF THE VELD. The Life of Bishop Key.

By **Godfrey Callaway (Priest), S.S.J.E.**, the author of 'Sketches of Kafir Life,' &c.

Illustrated from photographs supplied by the author.

With a Map. **2s. 6d.** net. [*Second Edition.*

A very remarkable record of a remarkable work in South Africa. A life which cannot fail to move even those who do not follow closely the work of the Church for the Empire.

'We can thoroughly recommend this book as a study of the missionary work close at hand, and as a record of a devoted and saintly Bishop whose works are following him.'
CHURCH TIMES.

THE LIFE AND TIMES OF MRS. SHERWOOD.

Edited by **F. J. Harvey Darton**. [*Second Edition.*

With Photogravures and other Illustrations. **16s.** net.

Mrs. Sherwood's life (1775–1851) gives a vivid account of England under George III., with scenes among the French emigrés, wanderings in France and Germany during the Revolution, and camp life in England and India.

'I do not know where you will get a more lively or living picture of middle-class English or Anglo-Indian life. . . . It is a high but just compliment to pay a volume of five hundred closely printed pages to say that you wished it longer.'
TRUTH.

'A mine of pure gold.'
GUARDIAN.

Biography—*Continued.*

ONE LOOK BACK.

10s. 8d. net.

By the **Right Hon. George W. E. Russell.**

'Everybody who is anybody' will have to read this volume. Of late years, Mr. Russell has contented himself with drawing upon his stories of anecdote and history for various scattered purposes. But in 'One Look Back' he tells to some extent the continuous story of his life and of the great changes in society and politics he has seen. It is practically an autobiography.

'Of fascinating interest . . . One of the best contributions to "reminiscence literature" that the season is likely to give us, both for the inherent interest of its matter and the charm of its manner.' DAILY TELEGRAPH.

'There is an abundance of good stuff in this volume—sketches drawn from the life, words of wisdom or folly remembered and here set forth, light and genial gossip, amusing persiflage—random, but not ineffective recollections.' DAILY NEWS.

Belles-Lettres.

MRS. FULLER MAITLAND'S NEW BOOK.

BY LAND & BY WATER.

6s.

By **Ella Fuller Maitland,** author of 'The Day-book of Bethia Hardacre,' joint author of 'The Etchingham Letters.'

A new book somewhat on the lines of the charming 'Day-book of Bethia Hardacre.' A work which can be read and re-read at all times and in all places.

'The charm of Mrs. Fuller Maitland's matter is in the manner of the telling.' SPECTATOR.

Travel.

A BISHOP AMONGST BANANAS:

Or, Work and Experiences in a Unique Diocese.

By the **Right Rev. Herbert Bury, D.D.,** Bishop of British Honduras and Central America; with Letters of Introduction by the Bishop of London and Col. Roosevelt.

Illustrated from unique Photographs. **6s.**

Bishop Bury is a Churchman, and writes of the Church's work. But he is first and foremost a man, and no book of travel and exploration could be more fascinating than this record of journeys made in the footsteps of Drake, Morgan, and the Conquistadores. The book has an immediate practical bearing on certain world-questions like the Panama Canal, the extinction of malaria, and the colour problem.

'Dr. Bury's experiences have been varied and many, dangerous as well as delightful, instructive as well as amusing. He has given an account of a "unique Diocese," admirably written.' MORNING POST.

The Best Fiction.

THE ROUGH WAY.

By **W. M. Letts.** 6s.

'The Rough Way' is the story of a man who hesitates at the cross-roads of life. With George Herbert he knows 'the ways of pleasure ... the propositions of hot blood and brains;' and with the poet he sees, too, that there is another way, a rougher, lonelier way that leads to the stars. Inclination and his love for another, a frank hedonist, suggest the pleasant way. But circumstances may over-rule a man's choosing, and bar the road he would follow, and he may find his feet set on the 'Rough Way.' The story has no hero and heroine. It tells of the failures and mistakes of very fallible people.

'The Rough Way' has many charms. One of these is its utter freshness. . . . The book remains an achievement which will cause us to look for the keeping of her pen from any work that is not as finely wrought, as pure in heart.'
NATION.

'A study of the inner life of such intimacy and insight as to call for particular praise. . . . "The Rough Way" is of outstanding merit. . . . she emphasizes a fundamental truth which calls for emphasis at the present moment. . . . But from whichever point of the compass this book comes, it is a fine, clear study of the English Catholic position. But that is not all. It is a study of the way in which human beings are to find their souls. . . . The book is simply packed with observation.'
THE CHURCH TIMES.

WHEN THE SHADOWS FALL.

5s. net.

By **Elisabeth Eaton.**

'When the Shadows Fall' is a book which by its very simplicity of language and thought makes a direct appeal to every class of reader. It is the story of one whose life was marred by a great sadness, and of how human nature can emerge unconquered from great trial and suffering. Much of the book, as will easily be guessed, is based upon 'Elisabeth Eaton's' own practical experience.

'Sketched with so much sympathy that the ring of sincerity, essential in a book of this kind, pervades its pages. . . . We can whole-heartedly congratulate Miss Eaton, and shall look forward with pleasure to her next essay in the fields of literature.'
MORNING POST.

John Masefield.

JIM DAVIS.

6s.

By **John Masefield,** author of 'Captain Margaret,' 'Martin Hyde,' &c.

A romance of Smuggling in the Eighteenth Century. With remarkable unanimity reviewers hail this new work as Stevensonian in spirit and in execution — in fact worthy of R. L. S. at his best.

'A book that would have delighted Stevenson.'
PUNCH.

G. K. Chesterton.

THE BALL &
THE CROSS.

6s.

[Second Issue.

A philosophic romance in which Mr. Chesterton deals inimitably with problems of faith and doubt.

'Far more good solid work than in any of Mr. Chesterton's previous essays in fiction.'
PALL MALL GAZETTE.

Architecture.

PORCHES AND FONTS.

Their Liturgical Uses and Architectural Beauties.

By **J. Charles Wall. 10s. 6d. net.**

All lovers of Archæology and old churches will be interested in the carefully compiled work, which is finely illustrated by the author.

In writing this book, Mr. Wall has travelled all over the country collecting material, and the result is a volume which will prove of the greatest interest to every one for whom the subject has the slightest attraction.

'We have nothing but praise for the wealth of material relating to 'Porches' that Mr. Wall has gathered; the illustrations, all by the author, are numerous, and carefully drawn with a delicate touch.'
ATHENÆUM.

'The descriptions and pictures of the sculpture, moulding, flush-work, and other beautiful details of porches of the successive periods of Ecclesiastical art are delightful, and testify to a wide acquaintance with England's best example.'
CHURCH TIMES.

TOWERS AND SPIRES.

Their Design and Arrangement.

By the **Rev. E. Tyrrell Green, M.A.,** Lecturer in Theology and Hebrew, St. David's College, Lampeter ; sometime Scholar of St. John's College, Oxford.

With over 120 Illustrations. Cloth **10s. 6d.** net.

A work for all students of architecture as well as for cultured readers who take a living interest in their native land. Prof. Tyrrell Green lays special stress on the way in which local conditions have modified the architect's handiwork.

'A labour of love to which the writer has devoted eight or ten years is pretty sure to be interesting. It is so with the present book. . . . Professor Green deals ably with this period, and his treatment of the Gothic period raises a point of considerable interest.'
MORNING POST.

Sociology.

MARRIAGE AND THE
SEX PROBLEM.

5s. net.

By **Dr. F. W. Foerster,** Special Lecturer of Zurich University.
Translated by MEYRICK BOOTH, Ph.D.

Writing from the standpoint of the psychologist and educator, the author comes to the conclusion that the Christian Marriage Ideal best answers the physical, ethical, and spiritual needs of humanity. There is a section dealing with the education of boys and girls, and, in the opinion of many of the first educators of the day, this belongs to the very best literature that has appeared on this difficult subject.

'One of the most satisfactory books on this question. . . . A work that may be put into the hands of a young man or woman who should find in this volume a clear and definite discussion of matters that affect the race as well as the individual.' T.P.'s WEEKLY.

'An able defence of the Christian ideal of marriage. Thirty thousand of this book has been sold in Germany.' SCOTSMAN.

An Original Book on a new plan. The Illustrations are artistically mounted on brown paper.

THE MIGHTY ARMY.

5s. net.

By **W. M. Letts.** Illustrated in Colour by **Stephen Reid.** Fancy paper boards, with Coloured Medallion.

This handsome and attractive volume deals with the story-lives of great Christian leaders like St. Columba, St. Augustine, Thomas Becket, William of Wykeham, St. Hilda, Stephen Langton, Bishop Ken.

'The author merits the highest praise for this beautiful collection of stories from early Church history. It is one of the finest books of the season. The illustrations are ably arranged, giving the actors of the story in one picture, and the Cathedral or scene of the story in another. It is a book any grown-up will appreciate besides children from ten upwards.' BRITISH WEEKLY.

Uniform with this Volume.

THE ANIMAL
WHY BOOK.

5s. net.

[Third Edition.

By **W. P. Pycraft, F.Z.S., A.L.S,** Illustrated in Colours by **Edwin Noble, R.B.A.**

A book of Natural History on novel and interesting lines.

'One of the cleverest and most desirable picture books published this year.' GUARDIAN.

PADS, PAWS, AND CLAWS.

5s. net.

By **W. P. Pycraft, F. Z. S., A. L. S.** Pictures in Colours by **Edwin Noble, R.B.A.**

A New Fine Art Series.

CARAVAN TALES.

5s. net.

Adapted from the German of Hauff and others by **J. C. Hornstein.** Illustrated in Colours by **Norman Ault.** Fancy cloth boards.

A most attractive volume, which may be regarded either as a fine art gift-book or as a volume of exciting romance. Illustrated in colour by Norman Ault, the reproductions being mounted on toned paper.

'We rank this very high among gift books.' GUARDIAN.
'Will be welcomed with joy. Hauff's stories are nothing like so well known as they might be, and this collection should do much to bring them into rightful appreciation.' TRUTH.
'A capital book. . . . should easily take a front rank in this year's output of gift books.' FIELD.

Books for the Nature Lover.

THE SLOWCOACH.

Cloth, **6s.**
[*Second Edition*

By **E. V. Lucas.** Illustrated in Colours by **M. V. Wheelhouse.**

All those who are making plans for their holidays should read these caravan experiences.

'A most delightful story, and we recommend it with all our heart.' SPECTATOR.

A BOOK OF DISCOVERIES.

Cloth, **6s.**

By **John Masefield,** author of 'Captain Margaret,' &c. Profusely Illustrated by **Gordon Browne, R.I.**

No boy after reading this interesting volume can fail to use his powers of observation to read in the present the history of the past.

'It contains a wealth of information on all sorts of subjects that the boy wants to know about. It is indeed a delightful volume.' TRUTH.

THE DOG-LOVER'S BOOK.

Cloth, **15s**. net.

Pictures in Colour by **Edwin Noble, R.B.A.** With Preface by **Major Richardson.**

A full description of every kind of dog from every point of view, with many practical suggestions for dog-lovers.

'The most delightful book on "man's best friend" that we have seen this many a year. A most original and scholarly account of the different breeds.'
MORNING POST.

A Standard History.

THE KING'S BUSINESS.

3s. 6d. net.

By **F. Arnold-Forster.**

[*Third Edition, with additions.*

' *The King's Business' is the work of going into all lands and spreading His message. Miss Arnold-Forster tells the whole story of Christian Missions with authority, with originality, and with literary charm.*

'Should not only be in every Church library, and on every priest's shelves, but diligently circulated amongst all reading laymen. The style of the book is entertaining, there is not a dull page in it, and no words are wasted in mere moralisings. Boys who love adventure books will find satisfaction in most of the chapters, whilst girls with real interest in life will feel inspired to do something.' CHURCH TIMES.

A New Series of Copyright Novels.

THE WHITE LIBRARY.

1s. net each.

1. **A Princess of the Gutter.** By **L. T. Meade.**
   Fourth Edition.

2. **Three Girls in a Flat.** By **Ethel F. Heddle.**
   Third Edition.

3. **Mary Gifford, M.B.** By **L. T. Meade.**

4. **I Lived as I Listed.** By **A. L. Maitland.**

5. **Marget at the Manse.** By **Ethel F. Heddle.**

6. **Where the Brook and River Meet.** By **N. Hellis.**

7. **The Fiddlestring.** By **R. H. Bretherton.**

Lightning Source UK Ltd.
Milton Keynes UK
UKHW010631141118
332315UK00011B/1252/P